THROUGH THE YEAR WITH FULTON SHEEN

THROUGH THE YEAR WITH FULTON SHEEN

Inspirational Selections for Each Day of the Year

Compiled by Henry Dieterich

IGNATIUS PRESS   SAN FRANCISCO

Cover design by Riz Boncan Marsella

Published in 2003 by Ignatius Press, San Francisco
ISBN 0–89870–873–7
Library of Congress control number: 2003105175
Printed in the United States of America ∞

CONTENTS

INTRODUCTION

"My dear friends in Christ and him crucified"—thus Fulton Sheen began his homily on one of the last Good Fridays of his life. Christ was always the center of Archbishop Sheen's life, and as that life of service to the gospel of Christ grew nearer to its culmination, the cross took more and more the central place. In his autobiography, Archbishop Sheen recounts how his love of Christ overcame what he calls "staurophobia"—fear of the cross. He calls the crucifix his true autobiography, reflecting his heartfelt union with the crucified Savior.

From his boyhood in Peoria, Illinois, Fulton Sheen desired to serve God as his priest. From his days as a graduate student at the University of Louvain, the basic vocation of the priesthood was joined to the vocation that was to shape his life: to spread the gospel and lead men and women to Christ. In season and out, he proclaimed the good news of salvation: his converts ranged from high-ranking communists to the poor and humble. As U.S. national director for the Society for the Propagation of the Faith, he was no deskbound missionary, but took time to seek out and instruct new Catholics. His use of television and radio introduced these media into Catholic evangelization.

These two themes—devotion to the cross and evangelism—run through this collection of readings. They are drawn from talks by Archbishop Sheen that have never before appeared in book form. Many come from the final talks and homilies of his life; others from talks designed for the instruction of new Catholics.

The readings are arranged here, not necessarily in the order they appeared in the original talks, but with some attention to the seasons of the liturgical year. The months of February and March introduce themes appropriate for Lent; consideration of the Passion follows, and after that the meaning of Christ's Resurrection from the dead. The month of May begins appropriately with meditations on the Blessed Virgin Mary, followed by reflections on Christ's ascension and on the person and work of the Holy Spirit. Similarly the Advent and Christmas seasons have suitable readings.

Many of the talks from which these readings were drawn were originally sermons for Good Friday and Holy Week. Therefore the reader will discern in many of the meditations an underlying orientation toward the Passion of Christ. Since this mystery is at the center of our redemption, remembrance of the Passion is appropriate to any season of the year. To consider the theme of Christ's redemptive suffering and death, moreover, is to touch the heart of Archbishop Sheen.

These readings are presented that you too may draw closer to the cross of Christ. It is not only to unbelievers that the gospel must be preached. In living the life of Christ, we never outgrow the need for faith in the gospel; we never outgrow our need for the cross. Indeed, our life should bring us closer and closer to the cross of Christ, so that we can say with Archbishop Sheen, "The crucifix is my autobiography."

Henry Dieterich

January

Christianity is Christ

The founder of no other religion is absolutely essential for that religion in the same way that Christ is essential for Christianity. It is true that the founder was necessary for the founding, but the believer in a particular religion does not enter into the same kind of an encounter that a Christian enters into with Christ. It is the personal relationship to him which is decisive. Christ therefore occupies a different place in Christianity than Buddha does in Buddhism, than Confucius in Confucianism, Muhammad in Islam, and even Moses in Judaism. When you come to Christ, Christianity demands the personal, intimate bond. We have to be one with him, one with him in such a way that we cannot in any way claim to be Christian unless we reflect the person, the mind, the will, the heart, and the humanity of Christ.

What faith really is
January 2

Faith is not a wish to believe or a will to believe something contrary to reason. Faith is not living *as if* something were true. Faith is the acceptance of a truth based on the authority of God's revelation, as manifested in the Church and in scripture. God alone causes faith in the believer, and faith is not the acceptance of abstract ideas. It is so often said, "Oh, by faith you have to accept a number of dogmas." No! Faith is participation in the life of God. In faith, two persons meet:

God and ourselves. Our affirmation of faith does not come because we see a truth very clearly. But it comes from the vision of him who reveals that truth—and we know that he cannot deceive nor be deceived.

What is reconciliation?   *January 3*

Reconciliation is inseparable from the death of Christ. That is important to understand. In other words, we never have reconciliation without the Passion, death, and Resurrection of our Lord. For example, Romans 5:10: "For if we were God's enemies, we were reconciled to him through the death of his Son." Again 2 Corinthians 5:14: "For the love of Christ leaves us no choice, when once we have reached the conclusion that one man died for all and therefore mankind has died. His purpose in dying for us was that all men, while still in life, should cease to live for themselves, and should live for him who for their sake died and was raised to life." Then again in Colossians 1:22: "But now by Christ's death in his body of flesh and blood God has reconciled you to himself so that he may present you before himself as dedicated men without blemish and innocent in his sight." Reconciliation therefore comes through redemption.

Because of sin we need a fresh start   *January 4*

Imagine a great orchestra on a stage. The conductor is before his musicians, and every one of the musicians has music before him, well scored. They are all skilled, but free. One of the musicians decides to strike a sour note. In the face of that discord the director might strike his baton and say, "Play it over." But it makes no difference because that sound is traveling out into space at the rate of about twelve hundred feet a second—and on and on that discord goes. So long as the universe endures there is disharmony. Is there any way to stop it? Not in time, for time is irreversible. It could, however, be stopped if someone reached out from eternity and grabbed that wild note in its mad flight. Then it would no longer be a disharmony, or rather it would be stopped from spoiling the harmony of the universe. But would it still be a discord? Yes, except on one condition. Suppose that he who stopped it wrote a new symphony and made that sour note the first note in the new melody. Then it would be a sweet note. That is what happened to mankind. Man was free. He struck a sour note, and that sour note infected all humanity. How could we ever have harmony in the universe again? God reached out and raised up a man who was untouched by that sour note—thanks to the Immaculate Conception and the virgin birth—and he started a new humanity.

Christ overcame all our evils   *January 5*

There are three kinds of evils in the world: physical, mental, and moral. Physical evil includes sicknesses and illnesses. Mental evil includes retardation, agnosticism, doubt, and skepticism. Moral evil includes sin. Our Lord transferred to himself all of these evils, first of all physical ills. St. Matthew, quoting Isaiah, says: "He took upon himself our sicknesses and our illnesses." We have no record that our Lord was ever sick, and I'm sure that he never was because no one could touch him physically until he said *now* the night of the Last Supper when Judas went out of the door. His enemies attempted to throw him over the brow of the hill, and three times they tried to arrest him. But even stonings went amiss. If then, our Lord suffered no physical ills, how could he take upon himself our sicknesses and our illnesses? By empathy. Jesus had such a deep sympathy and unity with the sufferings of mankind that he felt them as his own. A mother feels the evil of her delinquent daughter much more than her daughter does. The father of the prodigal son who waited on the road suffered more than the prodigal son. And our Lord, therefore, took on himself all physical illnesses to such a degree that when he worked miracles by healing the deaf and blind, as Mark tells us, he sighed. He groaned. He wept. Three times he wept—over a decadent civilization, over death, and over sin, as the epistle to the Hebrews says. I'm sure that our Blessed Lord felt the blindness of a Milton and the deafness of a Beethoven and the isolation of a leper.

Christ overcame sin   *January 6*

Moral redemption from sin was the principal reason Jesus came. Mental and physical evils are consequences of moral evil because they came into the world as the result of a rebellion against God. So now Jesus assumes our guilt as his own. That was why he was silent seven times before Pilate. Seven times he took our place, when we deserved to be condemned. Seven times he spoke as the shepherd, seven times silent as the lamb. During World War II on the Burma Road the Japanese had some prisoners. At the end of a working day one shovel was missing. The Japanese commander said that if the shovel was not returned within five minutes, ten men would be shot. It was not returned at the end of three minutes. They repeated the warning. One man stepped forward and was clubbed to death. When they got back, they found all the shovels. Like Jesus, the dead prisoner had taken on the guilt of others.

Do not pass by this great salvation   *January 7*

Love of man is God's hell. Our Lord had a hell, and it was because he loved us. Love of mankind was Christ's hell.

So in these days when the word "reconciliation" has become popular, let us not reduce it to sociological reconciliation, political reconciliation, or any other kind of reconciliation until we have first sounded the profound depths of this great mystery. The word "reconciliation" is never mentioned in scripture apart from the death of Christ.

> I slipped his fingers, I escaped his feet.
> I ran and hid for him I feared to meet.
> One day I passed him, fettered on the tree.
> He turned his head and looked and beckoned me.
> Neither by speed nor strength could he prevail,
> each hand and foot was pinioned by a nail.
> He could not run, nor clasp me if he tried,
> but with his eyes he bade me reach his side.
> For pity's sake, thought I, I'll set you free.
> "Nay take this cross," said he, "and follow me.
> This yoke is easy, this burden light,
> not hard nor grievous if you wear it tight."
> So did I follow him who could not move,
> an uncaught captive in the hands of love.

Less of me, more of Christ   *January 8*

The coach of the Oakland Raiders said to me one day, "What are you teaching in Catholic colleges? I have players come to me saying, 'I've got to do my thing.' How are we going to have a football team if everybody does his thing? I thought Christian charity meant doing the other person's thing." And so we become wild and confused and full of psychoses and neuroses as soon as the *I* begins to get in the way.

I don't want my life to be mine, I want to be Christ's. The more ego there is, the less there is of Christ. If the box is full of salt, you cannot fill it with pepper. And if we're filled with the search for identity, we are not identical with Christ. The more we are Christ, the more he can use us. And he does not use us, he does not open doors and give us opportunities, until we are flexible in his hands, obedient like a pencil. If I want this pencil to write God, it writes God. But let this pencil be endowed with its own will, when I want to write the word God, it writes the word dog. I can't do anything with it. So the effectiveness of our apostolate depends to a great extent upon denial of self and the search to be one with Christ in knowledge and in will. Then after a while we reach a point where nothing in all the world is worth a moment of time except to know more of him.

Wooden Christ or living Christ?   *January 9*

St. John Adcock wrote a poem contrasting a child playing with a wooden lion and a Christian. He wonders what would happen if the wooden lion ever came to life, and what would happen to the Christian if Christ appeared.

When a blithe infant wrapped in careless joy
sports with the wooden lion, if the toy
should come to life, the child so direly crossed
faced with this actuality were lost.
Leave us our toys then, happier we shall stay
while they remain but toys and we can play
with them and do with them as suits us best.
Reality would add to our unrest.
We want no living Christ whose truth intense
and flashing on all folly and deceit
would blast our world to ashes at our feet.
We do but ask to see no more of him below than is
    displayed

in the dead plaything our own hands have made,
to lull our fears and comfort us in loss
the wooden Christ upon the wooden cross.

Forgotten is the reality of Christ who chose a human nature and continues his Incarnation by choosing ours. He wants us, therefore, to be available so that he can display his power through us, his truth through us.

The Christian is another Jesus   *January 10*

A friend of mine, a priest, spent fourteen years in a communist prison and was tortured intensely because he always preached Christ to the prisoners. When he was released, he met a boy on the street and said to him, "Do you believe in Christ?"

"No," said the little boy, "I don't."

"Why not?"

"Well, you believe that Jesus is God, don't you? If Jesus is God, he ought to be able to do many things. God made elephants. Elephants make other elephants. God made trees, and trees make other trees. God made flowers, and flowers make other flowers. If Jesus is God, therefore, he ought to be able to make other Jesuses. But I have never seen another Jesus. My father was an alcoholic; my mother takes in washing. She's never given me anything; no one has ever given me anything, so I don't believe that Jesus is God."

My friend went to another pastor in the village and told him what the boy had said. The pastor said, "Oh, that silly idiot of a kid." But he wasn't an idiot; he was right. If Jesus is God, he ought to be able to make other Jesuses. And that's what we are.

We have three different ways of living, only three. One, make your own self the guide of everything. Second, follow rules and commandments. Third, make Christ the law of life. First, be like Narcissus, who looked into the pool, saw his own image and fell in love with it. The first way of living says, I am the rule; I've got to be me; I've got to do my thing; selfishness; egotism. As Sartre, who was the philosopher of these people said, "My neighbor is hell." Why? Because he stands opposite me. The second way of living is to follow the commandments and rules of life. This is a very commendable way of living, but it is very difficult to fall in love with an abstraction. Honesty is the best policy, yes. We know what is right, but we sometimes lack the power to do what is right. Since there is no person involved, it becomes rather difficult to embrace the rule of life, something that is so far away from love itself. That brings us to the third way of governing our lives. That is: I will try to repay Christ's love for me by living his life. I know that he loved me, because he died for me, as if I were the only person in the world who ever lived. Because he died for me, I will do whatever he wants me to do. I will put on the Christ-mind. My actions will reflect Christ. I will speak about him when another heart is empty. I will dream about him. He is my dream, my love. When Christ becomes the rule of life, then his life becomes ours.

Absurdity   *January 12*

There are two ways of waking up in the morning. One is to say, "Good morning, God." And the other is to say, "Good God, morning." People who wake up the second way have an anxiety about life. It seems rather absurd. Considerable literature is being produced today on the absurdity of life. I suppose one of the best expressions of that absurdity occurred in a novel about a city on a river. In this particular novel there were two factories. One factory was on one side of the river and the other factory on the opposite side. The factory on one side of the river took great big stones and smashed and ground them to powder. Then, when the stones were reduced to powder, they shipped the powder to the other side of the river where the other factory turned the powder into great big boulders. Then the boulders were sent back to the first factory and so the routine continued. This was a literary expression of the way some people today regard life.

Saved from absurdity   *January 13*

When I first went to Europe to study as a young priest, I lived in a boardinghouse which belonged to a certain woman, whom we will call Madame Citroff. I was there about a week when she came to me and told me the tragic story of her family. After her marriage, her husband left her. A daughter that was born to them became immoral on the streets of Paris. Then Madame Citroff pulled out of her pocket a small vial of poison. She said, "I do not believe in God. Sometimes the thought comes to me that there is a God, and in case there be one, I curse him. So I've decided simply, because life has no meaning and is absurd, to do away with it. I intend to take this tonight. Can you do anything for me?"

"Well," I said, "I can't if you're going to take that stuff." So I asked her to postpone her suicide for nine days. I think it's the only case on record of a woman postponing her suicide for nine days. Well, I never prayed before in my life as I prayed for that woman. On the ninth day, the good Lord gave her great grace. Some years later, on the way to Lourdes,

I stopped off at a city where I enjoyed the hospitality of the Monsieur and Madame and Madamoiselle Citroff. And I said to the village curé, "Are the Citroffs good Catholics?"

He replied, "Oh, it's wonderful when people keep the faith all during their lives." He did not know the story.

Finding meaning in your neighbor   *January 14*

Not very long ago a father brought me his young son, a very self-wise, conceited young delinquent, who had given up his faith and was bitter with himself and everyone he met. The next day the boy ran away from home. He was away for a year. The boy came back as bad as ever, and the father brought him to me and said, "What shall I do with him?" I said, "Send him to school, but not in the United States." So I recommended a certain school to him, and about a year later the boy came back to see me. He said, "Would you be willing to give me moral support for an enterprise that I have undertaken in Mexico? There's a group of boys in the college I attend who have built a little school. We have gone all around the neighborhood and brought in the children to teach them catechism. We will also bring in a doctor from the United States once a year, for one month, to take care of all the sick people of the neighborhood." I asked him how he became interested in this work. "Well," he said, "the boys went down there during the summer, and I thought I would go down too." He recovered his faith and his morals and everything else, in his neighbor.

God works in mysterious ways   *January 15*

I remember once inviting to see me a woman who had just lost her eighteen-year-old daughter. She was very rebellious and had no faith whatever. She said, "I want to talk about

God." I replied, "All right, I will talk about him for five minutes, and then you talk about him or against him for forty-five, and then we will have a discussion."

Well, I was talking about two minutes and she interrupted me. She stuck her finger under my nose and said, "Listen, if God is good, why did he take my daughter?"

I said, "In order that you might be here, learning something about the purpose and meaning of life." And that is what she learned. She found it and discovered it.

Covering up conscience   *January 16*

A man of the theater came to see me a few years ago. His reason was this: one night after a show he was talking to a number of theatrical people backstage and they said to him, "You are a Catholic, aren't you?" And he said, "I used to be, but I've done considerable reading in comparative religion, psychology, psychiatry, and metaphysics, and I had to give it up. Nobody could answer my questions." Someone said, "Why don't you go to Bishop Sheen and have him answer your questions?" So he said, "Here I am, and I have a number of questions that I would like to put to you."

I said to him, "Now before you ask a single question, you go back to the hotel where you are living, get rid of that chorus girl you're living with, and then come back and ask the questions."

He threw up his hands and laughed, and he said, "Oh, certainly. I am trying to fool you just like I tried to fool myself. That's the reason."

I saw him not very long ago and I said, 'Well, you are still off the track, aren't you?"

"Yes," he said, "but I have not thrown away the map." Now here was a perfect example of someone covering up conscience.

Guilt will always come out; one can see it when one knows souls well. I was once instructing a young woman who had finished about fifteen hours of teachings on tape and records. After the first instruction on confession she said to my secretary, "I'm finished. No more lessons. I do not want to hear anything about the Catholic Church from now on."

My secretary phoned me and I said, "Ask her to finish the other three on the subject of confession, and then I will see her." I saw her at the end of these three, and she was in a veritable crisis. She was screaming, shrieking, "Let me out of here! Let me out of here! I never want to hear anything again about the Church after hearing this talk on confession."

Well, it took about five minutes to calm her down and I said, "Listen, my good girl. There is absolutely no proportion between what you have heard and the way you are acting. So there has to be something else. Do you know what I think is wrong? I think you have had an abortion."

She said, "Yes"—so happy that it was out. Now see how that bad conscience came out? She made an attack upon confession, the truth, the faith—but that was not the problem.

The gentle voice in the night   *January 18*

It is the conscience that tells us when we do wrong, so that we feel on the inside as if we have broken a bone. The bone pains because the bone is not where it ought to be. Our conscience troubles us because the conscience is not where it ought to be. Thanks to this power of self-reflection that we have, we can see ourselves, particularly so at night. As the poet put it, "Every atheist is afraid of the dark." It's a gentle voice, saying, "You are unhappy. This is not the way." Your freedom is never destroyed but you feel the sweet summons, and you ask why it is not stronger. It is strong enough if we would listen.

A divine invasion

A woman wrote to me about her brother, saying that he was dying in a hospital and that he had been away from the sacraments for about thirty years. She said he led not just a bad life, but he was an evil man. He did much to corrupt youth and circulated all manner of evil pamphlets among the young to destroy both faith and morals. His sister said that about twenty priests had called on him, and he threw them all out of the hospital room—"So will you please go." Last-resort Sheen, I am. I visited him this particular night and stayed about five seconds, because I knew that I would fare no better than anyone else. But instead of just making one visit, I made forty. For forty straight nights I went to see this man. The second night I stayed ten or fifteen seconds. I increased my visits by several seconds every night. At the end of the month I was spending ten to fifteen minutes with him. But I never once broached the subject of his soul until the fortieth night. That night I brought with me the Blessed Sacrament and the holy oils, and I said to him, 'William, you are going to die tonight."

He said, "I know it."

I said, "I'm sure you want to make your peace with God tonight."

He replied, "I do not. Get out."

I said, "I'm not alone."

"Who's with you?" he asked.

"I brought the good Lord along. Do you want him to get out too?" He said nothing. So I knelt down alongside of his bed for about fifteen minutes because I had the Blessed Sacrament with me. After the prayer, I again said, "William, I'm sure you want to make your peace with God before you die." He refused and started screaming for the nurse. So in order to stop him I ran to the door as if I were going to leave. Then I quickly came back. I put my head down alongside of his face on the pillow, and I said, "Just one thing, William. Promise me, before you die tonight you will say, 'My Jesus, mercy.'"

He said, "I will not. Get out." I had to leave. I told the nurse that if he wanted me during the night, I would come back. About four o'clock in the morning the nurse called, and she said he just died. I asked her how he died. "Well," she said, "about a minute after you left he began saying, 'My Jesus, mercy', and he never stopped saying it until he died." There was nothing in me that influenced him. Here was a divine invasion upon someone who had the faith once and lost it.

White grace and black grace   *January 20*

What form does this divine invasion take? It is an infection that gets into the soul. It is a grace, but up to this point we do not know exactly the meaning of the word "grace". There are two kinds of grace: white grace which makes us pleasing to God, and black grace in which we feel his absence. Most people in the world today feel his absence—really feel it, even the atheists. It is not man who is on the quest for God. It is God who is on the quest for man. He leaves us restless. The first question we have in the scripture is: "Man, where art thou?"

The secret of my power   *January 21*

When I stand up to talk, people listen to me; they will follow what I have to say. Is it any power of mine? Of course not. St. Paul says: "What have you that you have not received and you who have received, why do you glory as if you had not?" But the secret of my power is that I have never in fifty-five years missed spending an hour in the presence of our Lord in the Blessed Sacrament. That's where the power comes from. That's where sermons are born. That's where every good thought is conceived.

I don't mean to say that these hours have always been good. I've had to walk up and down the church to stay awake. I once went into St. Roch's Church in Paris to pray an hour, when I had only two hours in Paris between trains on my way to Lourdes. There were only about five days a year when I could sleep in the daytime, and this was one. I sat down at two o'clock, and I slept perfectly until three. When I awoke I said to the good Lord, "Did I make a holy hour?" And my angel said, "Yes, that's the way the apostles prayed the first one."

Prayer drives out sin   *January 22*

One of the first effects of praying a daily holy hour will be to get rid of any evil that is in our life. Evil is not always to be overcome by combatting it directly. St. Paul even suggests that certain types of mortification do not do away with certain sins. How do we get rid of evil? By the expulsive power of a new affection. We do not drive out evil, rather we crowd it out. We drive it out when we attack it directly. We crowd it out when we bring something else in. It's like a man who leads an evil life until he meets a fine woman who leads him in the path of virtue. So St. Paul says: "Be not overcome by evil but overcome evil with good." How do we know for example that water is polluted? We know it from clean, clear water. Why are we shocked at bad grammar? Because we know good grammar. Why are we shocked at bad music?

23

Because we know harmonious music. Our spiritual life must not start with a deep consciousness of our guilt and sin. No. It is Christ that gives us a consciousness of guilt. He is first. Then we become aware of the fact that we have sinned against him.

We need to fall in love with the Lord   *January 23*

There was a priest who had a high office in one diocese. He was removed from office principally because of alcoholism. He went to another diocese but continued to give scandal. He happened to come into a retreat when I was talking about the holy hour, and he made the holy hour from that time on. He died in the presence of the Blessed Sacrament a month or two later. He had been battling drunkenness for years. But he overcame it in the end because of the expulsive power of the new affection. He fell in love with the Lord. Why do we not have zeal? Simply because we're not in love. Once we're on fire we'll do anything. When we love the Lord, we want to be with him. That is love's first effect.

Developing our spiritual senses   *January 24*

Another reason for praying the holy hour is that we need power. Power is born of silence and presence. As the Psalmist put it: "Be still and know that I am God." In prayer we shrug off the burdens of the world. We come in and spend an hour with the Lord and talk to him and listen and develop our senses of hearing and seeing and touching. Hearing: not doing all the talking. "Speak, Lord, thy servant heareth." Not listen, Lord, thy servant speaketh. And the Lord does talk to us.

Seeing: "The things that are temporal are seen", says Paul. We have a different vision before the Blessed Sacrament. Remember the priest and the Levite that passed by the wounded man on the road to Jerusalem. They did not want to see him because seeing created responsibility. There will be a shrinking from the Blessed Sacrament whenever there is not a good spiritual attitude in the soul. But when we heighten our spiritual vision, then we're doing something that the apostles had to do. They had to see beyond the veil of the flesh of our Lord in order to comprehend his divinity. And we have to see behind the veil of the species of bread to see his divinity as well. When we are used to seeing his divinity through the species of bread, then we will be better at seeing the image of God in people.

And finally, touch: touch is the mark of intimacy. Touch is communion. After many hours there begins to be a presence before the eucharistic Lord, a deep sense of oneness with Christ. We are even reluctant at the end of many an hour to leave the Lord. Like the disciples of Emmaus we say, "Stay with us Lord, the day is far spent."

The less of self, the more of Christ   *January 25*

The great battle the Church has to fight today is the affirmation of self. This stands in the way of God using us as an instrument. Look at the way the prophet Elisha handled a good woman who was suffering from considerable poverty. The wife of a member of the company of prophets appealed to Elisha: "My husband, your servant has died, and you know what a man he was. He feared the Lord, but a creditor has come to take my two boys as slaves." Elisha said to her, "How can I help you? Tell me what you have in the house." "Nothing at all," she said, "except a flask of oil." "Go out then", he said, "and borrow vessels and pots from all your neighbors. Get as many empty ones as you can and when you come home, shut yourself in with your sons and pour from the flask into these vessels, and as they are filled, set them aside." She left him and shut herself in with her sons, and they brought her the pots. She filled them, and when they were all full she said to one of her sons, "Bring me another pot." "There is not one left", he said. And the flow of the oil ceased. Why is it that some of us have more of Christ than others? Is it because Christ cannot get in? The more empty of self we are, the more he can fill us.

How God forms us   *January 26*

To learn how the Lord forms us as pots, we turn to the prophet Jeremiah. "These are the words which came to Jeremiah from the Lord: 'Go down at once to the potter's house and there I will tell you what I have to say.' So I went down to the potter's house and found him working at the wheel. Now and then a vessel he was making out of the clay would be spoilt in his hands, and then he would start again and mold it into another vessel to his liking. And then the word of the Lord came to me: 'Can I not deal with you, Israel, says the Lord, as the potter deals with his clay?'"

What the potter intended to do was to make a Ming vase. So here is the potter with the clay and the wheel, and he intends to make the best. And the clay somehow or other hardens, perhaps too rapidly, or it doesn't harden sufficiently and it falls down from the wheel. Does the potter neglect the clay? No, he picks it up and molds it into another vessel. God does not abandon us poor pots, he picks us up and makes us according to his liking, whatever it happens to be. We are not abandoned. But he does have an ideal just the same.

Here we come to a lesson that God teaches us concerning our treasure. The treasure we hold in our earthen pot is grace. We turn here to the prophet Jeremiah in the forty-eighth chapter: "All his life long Moab has lain undisturbed, like wine settled on its lees, not emptied from vessel to vessel; he has not gone into exile. Therefore the taste of him is unaltered, and the flavor stays unchanged."

Jeremiah is here describing the way the Jews made wine. They would pour the grape wine into a vessel, allow it to settle, and when the lees (the dregs) began to form, then the wine would be poured into another vessel. After the dregs had settled there, it would be poured into still another, and still another, and another, until it was perfect wine. God says here of Moab, the people that did not allow the Israelites to pass through their land, "Moab has settled on its lees." Moab never went into exile. There was no pouring out of a vessel, no change, no taking on of a new challenge, and for that reason it lost its taste. This is the reason we should make a daily holy hour, so that we'll not settle on our lees. The rest of our life we'll consider as dregs. Now we'll begin to be poured from vessel to vessel in order to be enriched with grace.

The battleground of the Church today *January 28*

The world in which we live is the battleground of the Church. I believe that we are now living at the end of Christendom. It is the end of Christendom, but not the end of Christianity. What is Christendom? Christendom is the political, economic, moral, social, legal life of a nation as inspired by the gospel ethic. That is finished. Abortion, the breakdown of family life, dishonesty, even the natural virtues upon which the supernatural virtues were based, are being discredited. Christianity is not at the end. But we are at the end of Christendom. And I believe that the sooner we face up to this fact, the sooner we will be able to solve many of our problems.

The challenge from our Lord   *January 29*

Thirty or forty years ago it was easy to be a Christian. The very air we breathed was Christian. Bicycles could be left on front lawns; doors could be left unlocked. Suddenly all this has changed; now we have to affirm our faith. We live in a world that challenges us. And many fall away. Dead bodies float downstream; it takes live bodies to resist the current. And this is our summons.

We will have to begin to be a different Church. We are for a moment on the trapeze. We are in between the death of an old civilization and culture and the swing to the beginning of the new. These are the times in which we live. They are therefore wonderful days, marvelous; we should thank God that we live in times like this.

The world is our testing-ground   *January 30*

At the [Second] Vatican Council, there was the discussion about the world. I remember one of the bishops from Belgium arose and made the proper distinction between the two uses of the word "world" in scripture. The word "world" can mean the theater of redemption, and in that sense it is good: "God so loved the world." But the world also means a spirit, an organization without God. So our Lord said, "I have taken you out of the world. Therefore the world will hate you." "I pray not for the world", he said. But there was a confusion. And the result is that today we have lost many of our faithful and our priests and our sisters, not because of christological heresy, nor because of persecution. The Lord has been very good to us; the only test he gave us was: "Will you become secular; will you leave?"

An army like Gideon's   *January 31*

The Lord is testing his Church. This testing is like the story of Gideon. Here's this great leader of the army of Israel, with an army of thirty thousand soldiers to do battle with an army of fifty thousand. What does God say to him? He said, "Your army is too great. Tell the cowards to leave." How many cowards were there? Twenty thousand: two out of three. God thins his ranks. Then he said to Gideon: "Your army is still too great, for if you win it would seem it was through your own power. Send them to the river and watch them drink." Some of them threw themselves prone on their stomachs and drank leisurely, comfortably, and to the full. Others ran along the bank, lapping up the water with their hands, and drinking in the fashion of dogs. And God said, "That's your army, three hundred, and I'll be with you." So God is thinning our ranks now as then, because we are preparing for a stronger and more holy Church.

February

God works through the minority

The Holy Spirit always works through minorities, never through majorities. Remember when Moses had just left Egypt with his Israelites, and he sent two of his trusted men, Caleb and Joshua, into the land of Canaan. He sent them with ten others—there were twelve spies in all—and he asked them to make inquiries about the army, the size of the cities, and so forth. They came back with a double report: a majority report and a minority report. The majority report of ten was, "We cannot take the land. The men there are so tall we look like grasshoppers beside them." Caleb and Joshua then spoke and said, "No, God said that we could take it." And the multitude turned on Caleb and Joshua and would have killed them had Moses not interceded. The majority was wrong; the minority with God can do anything.

We draw strength from our suffering brothers

Our Church today is a tested Church, in which we have to be better than we ever were before. We need to recognize that we are part of a very large mystical body that is all over the world, and that we who are weak, in this Western civilization, are drawing strength from great spiritual heroes in other parts of the world, particularly in Russia. What a great heart for Christ there is in that land, where one out of six has at least an indirect contact with Christianity! The bravery of their affirming the faith, the readiness to suffer for it!

The argument of holiness   *February 3*

In other parts of the world, our brothers in Christ are suffering for their faith. And here we are at ease, just undergoing a slight test and dividing our loyalty between Christ and the world. We must realize in minds and hearts that this is a new age, that we will have to be a creative minority, and that the only argument that is left to convince others is holiness. The world has heard every other argument, and it is ready to reject them all, all except one: holiness.

Does the crucifix mean anything to us?   *February 4*

This silver crucifix that I wear, I wear in reparation. I was in a Jewish jewelry store one day in New York, where I had known the jeweler for twenty or twenty-five years. He said to me, "I have some silver crucifixes for you." And he gave me a bag of silver crucifixes, over a hundred of them. I said, "Where did you get them?" "Oh," he said, "from sisters; they brought them in. They told me, 'We're not going to wear the crucifix any more; it divides us from the world. How much will you give us for the silver?'" The jeweler said, "I weighed them out thirty pieces of silver." Then he said, "What's wrong with your church? I thought that meant something to you." So I told him what was wrong. Three months later I received him into the Church.

Do not neglect so great a salvation   *February 5*

If a man takes a poison and is given an antidote, it makes no difference whether he throws the antidote out of the win-

32

dow or whether he just neglects it. Because the poison is operating in his system, death is certain. Scripture asks us, "How shall we escape if we neglect?"—just *neglect*. How often in the gospels, for example, it is said, "Thou didst not, thou didst not, thou didst not"—the refusal to walk the extra mile.

The mole once had eyes to see, but it grovelled down in the bowels of the earth, and Nature, as if seated in judgment, said, "Take the talent away!" And the talent that is not used was taken away. This is the first reason we have to begin to act differently, to resist the forces of evil.

Drawing closer to the light of Christ   *February 6*

Christ is our light; if we are walking away from the sun (for the sun is the symbol of Christ), the shadows are before us. This is one of the reasons why we have Catholics afflicted with every manner of psychosis and neurosis, afraid of these lengthening shadows, of these phantoms and fears and dreads. As we walk away from Christ, the further we go, the longer the shadows that appear before us—the resentment, the aggressiveness, just as soon as we are checked and told that we are walking from the light. If however, we walk toward the sun, and intensify our love of Christ, then all the shadows are behind us—all the remorse and regrets. As the sun comes more and more into our life, all these things pass away. Fears are gone, remorse is swallowed up in the intense love of Christ.

The danger of indifference   *February 7*

As time goes on, the good and the bad have different attitudes. The good are less conscious of their goodness. They strive to be zealous, close to the Lord; they're more conscious of their failings. But evil people, and those that are not living up to their full commitment to Christ, they're very satisfied. Samson did not know that his strength had left him. Saul, the first king of the Israelites, did not know that the Lord had left him. We can become self-satisfied and resent any challenge to change.

Take a frog; put that frog in water. Then heat the water imperceptibly, day by day increasing the temperature until the water is boiling. At no point during the increase of temperature will the frog ever offer resistance. It will never realize that the water is too hot—until it's dead. That's the way we are spiritually. We just become used to the temperature of the world. And we don't realize that it is gradually possessing us, until we are in its grip. So we are doing battle therefore with triteness, shallowness, and dullness, and we have to resist and begin to go in the other direction.

Do good people know they are good?   *February 8*

Truly good people are always unconscious of their goodness. Nothing embarrasses a spiritual person as much as to be told that he is spiritual. The closer we get to God, the less we are aware of being pleasing to God. Let me explain. If you take a painting and examine it by candlelight, the definitions seem rather good and the colors well chosen. But if you put it in the light of the sun, then all the defects stand out. When we compare ourselves with other people, we seem good; when we compare ourselves with God, we are nothing.

Has our love grown cold?   *February 9*

See how often sacred scripture indicates the decay of love among us. For example, the Jewish people had sworn to God that they would keep all the commandments, that they would accept the covenant, that they would do what God ordered them to do. They said the God of Israel would be their God. In six weeks they were prostrate before the golden calf. Moses turned and went down the mountain with the two tablets of the law in his hands. Joshua, hearing the uproar the people were making said to Moses, "Listen! There's fighting in the camp!"

Moses replied, "This is not the clamor of warriors or the clamor of a defeated people. It is the sound of singing that I hear." As he approached the camp, Moses saw the bull calf and the dancing, and he was angry. He flung the tablets down and they were shattered to pieces at the foot of the mountain. Then he took the calf that they had made and burnt it. He ground it to powder and sprinkled it upon the water and made the Israelites drink it. Then he said to his brother Aaron, the high priest, "Why did you do this?" This shows what happens when there's not strong leadership. "Why did you do this?" We can rationalize anything and here comes the lamest excuse that is recorded in all history.

Aaron said, "Well, I took the gold offerings that were given to me, I put it in the furnace, and it came out a calf." It came out a calf! And they said this was the god that led them out of Egypt. Love quickly decays.

Peter got wiser   *February 10*

The closer we get to Christ, the less certain we are of any merit of our own. Just study the way St. Paul characterizes himself in his epistles, in intervals of four, five, and six years between the letters. At first he says, "I am the chief of the apostles, I have labored more abundantly than any of them." He works a little longer and then he says, "I am not worthy to be called a member of the church, and the least worthy of all of the apostles." Finally, he ends up by calling himself the chief of sinners. St. Peter, too, became wiser; his first letter begins, "Peter, apostle of Jesus Christ". Here's a clear-cut affirmation of what he is. A few years later, Peter changes and he begins his letter, "Simon Peter"—Simon, poor weak human nature—"Simon Peter, apostle and *servant* of Christ".

February 11

The older we get, the better we see ourselves

When we're young, we think we're doing well. When we get older, we're sure we're not. Hence, when the adulteress was before our Lord, the woman whom the people wanted to stone, who left first, as Jesus wrote in the sand the sins of those who were there? The eldest: "They began to leave, beginning with the eldest." As we grow older, we know that we have done little service. I've been a priest for fifty-five years, for which I thank God. I was doing much better thirty years ago in my own mind than I am now. Now I feel as if I have done so little.

We can hate truth and fear goodness *February 12*

Evil works in us. Love declines. And then we hesitate about changing. St. Thomas says we can hate truth and fear goodness. We can hate truth because it means a change. For that reason we often resent the truth that is told about ourselves. We rationalize what we have done. We will stay away from a doctor, lest he find cancer. We do not want to know the truth. We like to hear about social action and political–moral problems, but we're not too keen on hearing the truth about ourselves. Truth hurts.

We fear goodness because we like to keep our own standards. We have moved away from the standard of Christ to the standard of the world. We do not ask ourselves, "Does this please Christ?" but "Does this please the world?" So I will dress and act in such a way that I will not be separate from the world; I want to be "with it". We marry this age, and we become a widow in the next one. We take on its verbiage, its fashions. This is one reason for so much instability in the Church today: the sand on which we are walking is shifting. We've given up the rock which is Christ.

Why did the strong man lose his strength?   *February 13*

Samson, the strong man, fell in love with a woman named Delilah. And the lords of the Philistines went up to the country to see her and said, "Coax him and find out what gives him his great strength, and how we can master him, bind him, and hold him captive."

And Delilah tried to find out what gave Samson strength, until finally he told her the secret. He said, "If my head were shaved, then my strength would leave me and I should become as weak as any other man." Delilah then told the Philistines. She lulled Samson to sleep on her knees and summoned a man, and he shaved the seven locks of Samson's hair for her, and they made him captive. And Samson's strength left him. But the strength was not in the hair, as is so often erroneously said. Samson had taken the Nazirite vow which committed him first to abstain totally from women and from strong wine. The growing of the hair was a symbol of that vow, so that the cutting of the hair was also the symbol of the breaking of the vow.

And then Delilah cried, "The Philistines are upon you, Samson."

He woke from his sleep and said, "I will go out as usual and shake myself." In other words, "I'm as strong as I ever was." He did not know that the Lord had left him.

We're not as strong as we were.

Ease the problem or cure it?

We fear Christ's goodness. I remember when I was a boy, if I had a toothache I would always go to my grandmother, never to my mother. I would go to my grandmother because she would get some oil of cloves and put it on my tooth and ease the pain. If I went to my mother, she would take me to the dentist, and the dentist would start probing about, and I was absolutely sure that he would find something wrong and inflict a little pain on me. I feared goodness. This is the psychology of our mediocrity.

Could you be a sinner?
February 15

A question that is worth asking in our American culture is this: "Are you sick or are you a sinner?" It is not very likely that you would call yourself a sinner in the modern age. Today people are sick. Are we going to a psychiatrist because we've committed adultery? Are we visiting a mental therapist because we're homosexual? Are we being treated by a psychologist because we've been dishonest? There are no sinners. We are not responsible; we are not guilty. We may have an Oedipus complex, an Electra complex; maybe our parents were poor, or we were raised on grade B milk, or there were not sufficient playgrounds in our neighborhood, but a sinner?—that we could never be.

He was made one with transgressors
February 16

Now why is our Blessed Lord on the cross at this particular moment? Why did he come to this earth? If you search the scriptures, you will find that there was only one reason why our Blessed Lord came: in order to do away with sin. He took our sins upon himself, as if he were guilty. All the prophecies about him, particularly in Isaiah, speak of him as being made one with the transgressors, identifying himself with sinners. How did he take sin upon himself? He is the new Adam. We have received an inheritance of weakness from the first Adam. Now the second Adam, Christ, came and started a new humanity. In order to do that, Jesus needed to blot out sin. So he became our stand-in, our representative. He takes our place as if he were guilty of blasphemy, as if he were the sinner.

The blood of Christ   February 17

Life had to be forfeited for our sins, and no life is more precious than that of God who became man. His blood was the blood of the God-man, and therefore he paid the infinite price. We were not bought with gold and silver, but with the precious blood of Christ. That is how our sins are forgiven, and that is why our Blessed Lord prayed for our forgiveness at the moment that he poured out his blood for us sinners. If you have faith in Jesus' sacrifice, now is the time to go to confession, to get rid of your sins. When the priest raises his hands in absolution over you, the blood of Christ is dripping from his fingers. We priests are hardly conscious of this great power. I think we would almost be shocked to death if we ever really realized it. But that is how the sin is absolved, by this blood of Christ

Forgiveness   February 18

One of the most exalted descriptions of forgiveness that I have ever read came from a Russian bishop who was sentenced to death by communist authorities in Russia. His last prayer for his executioners was this: "Heavenly Father, I offer up for the sins of these men and my own sins, the death of your Son. But I also forgive my executioners as you forgive me. And so on judgment day, when these men stand before you, the angels will ask, 'What charge is brought against these men?' There will be no one to charge them with guilt. They are already forgiven."

Thomas More at his death said something similar. There were a couple of fallen priests who came to see him, and he said, "I will ask the good Lord to forgive you, and then you will not be accused, but we will all meet very merrily in heaven."

The boy in the confessional   *February 19*

Even if we claim not to believe, we still experience the moral effects of guilt. Some years ago, one of the archbishops of France, the archbishop of Paris, was preaching a sermon in which he said, "Years ago, some boys came into Notre Dame Cathedral and stood outside a confessional box, and they bet one another, 'Who is brave enough to go in and make a mock confession? We will give ten francs to anyone who does it.' One boy said he would go in and make a mock confession. So he went in and made a mock confession, and he was given a penance. He came out and asked for the ten francs. They said, 'Well, you haven't said your penance. You must have received one. What is your penance?' So he walked up to the communion rail and knelt before a crucifix, and he raised his fist and he said to our Lord on the cross, 'You died for me, but I don't give a —.' He couldn't finish it." The archbishop concluded the sermon saying, *I am that boy.*

Rebellion and expiation   *February 20*

The great sin of the human race is rebellion. We are rebels against God. Let my upright finger stand for the will of God, and my horizontal finger stand for my will. As soon as I put the horizontal finger against the vertical, I have physically a cross. Both sin and rebellion demand not only forgiveness, but also expiation. Suppose you had the authority to command me. And you said to me, "Take three steps to your right."

Preferring to do my own thing, I take three steps to my left. Later, I regret my action, and I say to you, "Will you forgive me?"

You forgive me, but before I can start acting normally, I have to take three steps backwards. Where I put my foot down in egotism, I now have to put it down in humiliation. That's the *expiation*. Only then can I begin to obey.

Both God and man   *February 21*

There has to be some way of overcoming disobedience and rebellion. The one who overcomes this rebellion must be both God and man. He has to be man, otherwise he could not act in *our name*. If, for example, you are arrested for speeding, I cannot go into the court and say to the judge, "I will take his place and his punishment." The judge will say, "You have nothing to do with this case." So he who comes to atone for our rebellion must be human to act in our name. He must also be God in order that his actions will have infinite value, in order that he can redeem us.

                                               February 22
He learned obedience through what he suffered

How is disobedience overcome? The epistle to the Hebrews contains the answer to that mystery. Hebrews states that though Christ was God, he overcame our disobedience by obedience. He learned it in the school of suffering and, once perfected, became the source of eternal salvation for all who obey him. Son though he was, he learned obedience. You see, as the Son of God, he could not learn obedience, because he was equal to God. But when God became man, then he was capable of learning obedience existentially, experimentally, but not the way that we learn obedience. We learned obedience by discovering the consequences of disobedience. Many of us are old enough to belong to a generation that believed in spanking. Our parents gave us a pat on the back that was hard enough and low enough in order to make us learn who was the master of the house. But we also were burnt by matches. We learned obedience by suffering the consequences of disobedience. Now our Lord learned obedience in the school of suffering by discovering how much it cost to obey the Father's will, for example, the ridicule that he received, the opposition of men, politics, religion itself. Each affirmed its own will and caused him suffering.

How did the Father suffer?   *February 23*

What was the role of the Father as the Son learned obedience? Our theology doesn't say much about this. We learn that the Father gave his Son. He so loved the world that he sent his Son. Now think of any earthly father offering his own son, for example, who was injured by a criminal, in expiation for that criminal. There's probably no earthly father in the world who would do that. Yet the heavenly Father gave his Son. What did it cost him? Now of course he did not suffer exactly as we suffer. But did Abraham have some kind of suffering that intimated the suffering of the heavenly Father? While the Son was away did the heavenly Father "feel" like the father of the prodigal son? A Japanese theologian by the name of Katamuri wrote a book entitled *The*

Pain of God, in which he tried to bring out the "sufferings" of the heavenly Father in giving his Son. The Father was disturbed by the sins of the world. In any case, while we cannot quite divine what the heavenly Father endured, as it were, we know he gave up something, in our language.

We need to resolve to change   *February 24*

When we are young, we have physical and emotional energy, but we are very much opposed to the expenditure of spiritual energy. In middle age we drift; the old become fixed and settled and refuse to change. And in this day when there is so much affirmation of self, we have almost turned around the words of John the Baptist saying: I must increase, he must decrease. I must draw attention to myself, and he must suffer the eclipse and decline. T. S. Eliot said that when everyone is running toward a precipice, he who walks in the opposite direction seems to have lost his mind. So when we fall into a pattern of ordinariness, we are loath to change.

February 25
When the Church walks away from the cross

Many of us have seen the Loggia of Raphael. It contains thirteen different rooms with columns and a ceiling on which there are paintings, all rather typical of that period of the Church when she was in a decline: the Reformation. If you remember walking through the Loggia of Raphael, you'll remember seeing peacocks, foxes, and elephants. There are only four religious paintings: the transfiguration is the last one in the life of our Lord. There is no crucifixion. No cross. You will always know the dark days of the Church when there is a walking away from the cross of Christ.

It almost seems as if we have two kinds of churches. One is the church of evangelization. The other is the church of development. One is the church of individual sanctification and the other that of social action. One emphasizes contemplation and the other political directives. There is a division throughout the entire Western world as regards these two churches. Is the division justified?

Let us go to the Mount of Transfiguration for the answer. Our Blessed Lord took with him Peter, James, and John to the mount. When they arrived, Jesus became transfigured. We see the heavenly Father renew Jesus' commission to redeem the world. Peter, James, and John are awed by this. Peter, in fact, is so struck by it that he says, "Lord, it is wonderful to be here. Let us build three tabernacles. One for you, one for Moses, and one for Elijah" But scripture says, "He knew not what he said." Now remember, here is the Church. Here are three members of the apostolic body. This represents one Church. It represents those who would like everything to be rather calm, to enjoy the pieties and niceties of religion, to stand in the glare of the divine beauty, and to be a sharer in the vision and understanding of the Old Testament. It also represents part of the divine commission to redeem the world, even though it meant the death of the Savior. This is apt to be the older aspect of the Church. It is content with the vision. But our Blessed Lord said, "Let us go down the hill." He was reminding the disciples that there was no such thing as capturing that transient glory. "You'll have to go down this hill and you will find something else. Then you will climb another hill which will be Calvary, and then you will come to perfect glory. But not now."

When the Lord came down from the Mount of Transfiguration, we encounter another part of the Church. Nine apostles were trying to deal with a social problem. A distraught father who has a boy with mental problems comes into the picture. He is the symbol of every social problem and the symbol of every father's worry. The father goes to the Church and says to the Church: "Will you help this boy? This is not a religious problem that I have. It belongs to the social order. Heal him." The father comes to our Lord and says: "They could not drive the devil out of my son. Will you drive him out?" And our Blessed Lord said to the disciples, "How long must I suffer you?" This is the church of development; this is the church of social action. This is the church of economic and political order. This is the church of secularity. This is the church of involvement. As the other was the church of ecstasy, apartness, individual sanctification, joy, happiness, peace. When his disciples said, "Why can we not drive him out?" the Lord almost became intolerant of them. He said, "O ye of little faith. You have no faith. You are trying to build up a new world. That kind is driven out only by prayer and fasting."

Which church was right? Neither. And that's the modern world. Divide it as you please. Say the church on the mountain represents the old. Say the church in the valley represents the young. Both of them are ineffective. One sleeping, misinterpreting the Passion of Christ, trying to translate an emotion into a religion. The other was dealing with the hard facts of life. This is our divorce. Neither one was right. So if we are to build up a Church for this new age, we will have to begin by putting the two together, by returning to the very fundamental doctrine that the Word became flesh: first the spiritual, then the action.

Our modern world is very fond of passing the buck. That is to say, of denying responsibility. It began in the garden. Adam blamed Eve. When Adam was asked why he sinned, he said, "It was on account of the woman you gave me". You see, he did not say his wife. He blamed God: "On account of the woman *you* gave me". Eve blamed the serpent, and the buck was passed on. Aaron blamed the furnace for turning out the calf. Children blame their parents; people blame their pastors; pastors blame their curates; the curates blame their pastors. All blame their bishops, and bishops blame congregations. Psychiatrists and psychoanalysts blame the grandfathers and grandmothers. They blame the want of sufficient playgrounds. They blame bad instincts. No one is responsible, and so the buck is passed on. President Truman used to have a sign on his desk reading: "The buck stops here." But it did not. Where does the passing of the buck and the denial of responsibility cease? At the cross. There it ends. At last there's someone to blame.

The cross without Christ; Christ without the cross

If we could take Christ off the cross and put him over to one side, and then put the cross without Christ on the other side, we would have the picture of the world. Who picks up Christ without the cross? Our Western, affluent, Christian civilization. No discipline, no mortification, no cross, no self-denial. Who picks up the cross without Christ? Russia, China. The ascetic principle of Christianity has moved to the totalitarian states: discipline, order, law, commitment to a common end. But neither side has the answer. The crossless Christ is weak, effeminate, and can never save, because there is no mention of sin. The Christless cross allows Dachau, Auschwitz, the squeezing of the lives of individuals like so many grapes to make the totalitarian wine of the state. The world problem and our own personal problem is this: Will Christ find the cross before the cross finds Christ?

March

The discipline of pruning
March 1

Our Blessed Lord used a powerful simile when he talked to his apostles the night of the Last Supper. He said: "I am the real vine, and my Father is the gardener. And every barren branch of mine he cuts away and every fruiting branch he cleans to make it more fruitful still." So the heavenly Father purges us. A discipline, a trial, a handicap, or a cross comes into our life. And why is the pruning done? To make us more fruitful. That's why we've asked for this change, for more fruit. Our vines have to be pruned. We will be surprised at the richness of the harvest.

We need this discipline
March 2

Whether you use the analogy of changing from vessel to vessel so we do not settle on our lees, or of emptying ourselves in order that we might be filled (for God's grace stops when we are filled), or whether it be discipline so that we do not become bastards, the principle is the same. The cross has to be introduced into our lives. If we take on the discipline ourselves, the daily hour of prayer, the Lord will not have to empty the vessel of its lees or dregs. After we have embraced discipline, then we will be prepared to change others.

Avoiding the cross is the essence of the demonic. When finally our Lord was on the cross, Satan had one last chance to be anti-*crucial*. Through his agents he challenged the Lord, "Come down and we will believe." Believe? Sure. In what? The Trinity? Yeah, sure. In the hypostatic union? Yes. That he's the Son of God? Yes. That he made Peter the rock of his Church? Certainly. That he will send the Spirit? Sure. That he will rise from the dead? Sure. Anything—just come down and we will believe. Jesus did not come down. Had he come down, he never would have saved us. It's human to come down. It's divine to hang there. Consider the softness of the Church today: the desire to accommodate herself in the world, shrinking away from sacrifice, self-denial. We have today in the Christian world a new dirty word, but it doesn't have four letters. The new dirty word has five: c-r-o-s-s. Christ without the cross? Sure—anyone will accept that.

The answer to evil   *March 4*

What answer can we give or what consolation to someone in a concentration camp, to a mother with several children dying of cancer, a bereavement—what solace do we bring? What is the answer to the problem of evil? There was no answer until the Lord came down from heaven. He broke through this world of sin and evil; he entered into it and made it a part of himself. He identified himself with evil. Sinless, he was nevertheless made sin. A Nazi guard during the Nuremburg Trial said that he was sent in to burn hundreds of Jewish bodies, all naked and dead. When he went to set the fire, he saw in their midst one body clothed, that of a young girl of about eighteen. "Who are you?" "I am a Jewess from Salonika." "What are you doing here?" She said,

"Did you think that I could live when all my people are dying?" So this is the only answer that there is to the problem of evil. There's no other. Our Lord took it upon himself.

Peter and suffering   *March 5*

If there was one dominant characteristic about St. Peter, it was that he hated discipline, mortification, and self-denial. He's just like the rest of us. He wanted to lay hold of the immediate and that which is joyful, but he did not want to have anything really *crucial* in his life. That is evidenced first of all on the Mount of the Transfiguration. Here our Blessed Lord revealed himself in his risen glory when his face shone as the sun and his garments were as white as snow. While he was in this state, Moses and Elijah appeared. And what did our Lord talk to them about? His death. Peter all the while was asleep in a trance, and when he became conscious of the transfiguration, his first thought was: "Lord it's wonderful to be here." Let's capture this glow. This is the kingdom of God. The gospel says, "He did not know what he was saying." So our Lord later took him down the mountain where there was the father with the demonic child. Peter was to go to still another mountain, and only after climbing that mountain—Calvary—would he ever understand the glory that came after another, and very different, kind of transfiguration at Calvary. So Peter did not understand suffering.

Should we come down from the cross?   *March 6*

Two thieves were nailed on either side of our Lord. They both cursed and blasphemed; there was no difference between them at the beginning. The first one, the rebel that was on the left of our Blessed Lord represents the pain of those who say, "Take me down." The one on the right wanted to be taken up. The one on the left turned his head as much as he could and said to our Lord, "If you are the Son of God, save yourself; save us." He thought that our Lord was simply a healer. There are many today who are beginning to believe that this is the essence of Christianity—healing. The Lord does heal, but not always. There will not be a complete healing until the whole cosmos is renewed. Our Lord did not heal Lazarus, he allowed him to die. Our Lord did not release John the Baptist from prison. God does now and then heal. But healing is not the essence of his coming. That was all, however, that the rebel on the left wanted, just to be healed. As a matter of fact, if he were living today, he would probably never think of sin. If he had money, he would spend thousands of dollars on psychotherapy. But the thought of sin never entered into his mind—just the desire to be taken down.

The means of obtaining glory   *March 7*

There is only one way that pain can be handled, and that is by looking at this scene: the three crosses on Calvary and particularly our Blessed Lord in the middle. He took this absurd symbol of the cross, put himself upon it, and solved the enigma of life and death. He solved it by making a condition of life. "Take up your cross daily and follow me." Good Friday is the condition of Easter Sunday. The crown of thorns is the condition of the halo of light. The scourged body is the condition of the glorified body. You die with him, you rise with him. In other words, he conquered pain by using it as a means of attaining glory.

Has God ever suffered?   *March 8*

Does God know anything about pain? Does God know what
I suffer? Did God ever have a migraine headache, as if his
head was crowned with thorns? Does God know anything
about the wounded hands and feet that are brought in to the
accident wards of hospitals? Does God know anything about
the starvation in India and Africa? Did he ever go without
food for two days? Or three? Or five? Does he know anything about thirst? Does God know anything about home-
lessness? Was he ever without a home? Does he know what
it is to be a refugee? To flee from one country to another?
Does he know what it is to be in jail? To be the victim of
scourging? Does God know any of these things? Yes. God is
in Christ reconciling the world to himself.

Hands and feet and side   *March 9*

St. John, in his vision of heaven and the Lamb, pictures the
Lamb coming again on the last day to judge us. All will see
him, even those who have pierced him. He will come bearing the same scars that he showed to Thomas on his hands
and feet and side. Hands that broke bread to signify his own
broken body. Hands that ministered bread to the starving.
Hands that laid themselves on the heads of little children.
Hands that touched lepers. Hands that were calloused in the
carpenter's shop. Feet. Feet the mother worried about as they
pattered over lumber and nails and hammers, and brought
her visions of the man who would be put to death by the
same lumber and nails and hammers. Feet that Magdalen
would wash. Feet before which the Syrophoenician woman
threw herself in petition, in love. The wound in the heart. It
was large enough for a hand, for our Lord said to Thomas,
"Put your hand into my side." So when this Lamb comes,

bearing these signs on hands and feet and side, we will all see the scars. We will be judged by them. He will say, "Show me your hands. Have they been scarred from giving? Are they scarred in service? Are they scarred in labor? Are they scarred in relieving the cares of feverish brows? Have they been scarred in giving food to the hungry? 'For I was hungry and you gave me to eat.' Show me your feet. Have they gone on missions? Have they helped missionaries? Have they gone about doing good? Have they often made a track down the middle aisle of the church to visit the eucharistic Savior? Have they ever wandered to the feet of the crucifix? Show me your side. Is it scarred in pain out of love for him? Has the heart been scarred in love—not in need-love or self-satisfying love, but in gift-love? Is the side scarred from thinking about my Passion and my death that you may glory in my Resurrection?" This is the way you'll be judged: hands and feet and side.

We are all sinners   *March 10*

I once gave a retreat in a maximum security prison, where there were 1,979 inmates. All of them thought, of course, that I had on a white hat and they had on black hats, that I was good and they were bad. How could I begin? Well, I began by saying, "Gentlemen, I want you to know that there is one great difference between you and me. You got caught. I didn't." In other words, we are all sinners.

Brands plucked out of the burning   *March 11*

After seventy years of captivity in Babylon, 4,289 priests returned to Jerusalem. They were in rags, filthy, looking like anything but priests. At home there were the few who had stayed, and they were assisting Zerubbabel in the rebuilding of the Temple. Zechariah tells us that the high priest, the one who was chosen among them all, was brought before the angel of the Lord. And there stood the adversary, the accuser. That is what the devil is: he is that in the book of Job; he is that in the book of Revelation. And the accuser accused Joshua. "Look at his filthy garments! Look at that! Is that a priest?" And the angel of the Lord replied, "Is not this man a brand plucked out of the burning? Clothe him with new robes."

That's what we are. All brands plucked out of the burning.

Some unlikely saints   *March 12*

If at any time we are tempted to despair, simply because of the accuser, it is well to go back and pick up the eleventh chapter of Hebrews, which is the catalogue of the Old Testament saints. Read through that catalogue of saints sometime. Then go back and read the lives of those men and women in the Old Testament. They are all brands plucked out of the burning. Noah: he got drunk after the flood. Abraham: God told him to leave his country with his wife Sarah, and he took his nephew with him and his nephew's wife, whom God did not say to take, and they caused him trouble. He then went into Egypt when there was a famine, instead of trusting in God; then he sinned with Hagar, and out of this union came Ishmael. Yet Abraham is praised for his faith eleven times in one chapter of Hebrews. Moses killed a man. Samson, an adulterer, broke his vows as a Nazirite. Barak, general of an army, would not go to war, unless the woman Deborah went with him so he could lean on her military judgment. And so on through the scriptures. In the Old Testament they seemed to be entirely different characters. So God chose them not just because of what they were, but because of what they could become. That's why he chose us;

because we are his instruments. His power is shown by what he can do with reeds.

The old things that are good   *March 13*

One thing we must do is to recall the old things that were right. Consider the journey of our Lord on Easter Sunday afternoon. It was a seven-mile journey to the city of Emmaus, with the disciples. That was a trip we all would have loved to have made. During those seven miles, our Lord unfolded the scriptures: the law, the prophets, David—all the things that the disciples knew. Suddenly these things began to appear in a new light. So it is with us. The things that are old, that we know so well: the Trinity, Christ, the Eucharist—all these things have to come back to us and be discovered in their new beauty. We need to learn the lesson that the disciples had to learn when Jesus said to them, "Did you not know that the Son of Man must suffer in order to enter into his glory?" Notice that it was the *risen* Lord that spoke these words. That's the lesson we have to re-learn from Christ. He's our life; he's everything.

Did God make a mistake?   *March 14*

As we read over the gospels, particularly the first part of the gospel story, we sometimes feel that Jesus made a mistake in choosing Peter. Peter was impetuous, cowardly—making promises that he could never keep and did not intend to keep, even denying the Lord. Yet the Lord never said to him, "I told you. I told you you would fall." Never that. Our Lord was patient with Peter, and Peter became a saint. Our Lord did not make a mistake. Our Lord did not make a mistake in choosing any one of us. He knew what we would be, what we would become. Maybe we have not become all that he expected, but he knew the sanctity that was in us. What he said to Peter the week after the Resurrection, he says to us, "Simon, son of John, do you love me? Do you love me? Do you love me?" That question is answered in silence.

Mary and Christ's suffering   *March 15*

Mary's participation in Christ's suffering began with the annunciation, when she was asked to give God a human body, more properly, a human nature. In other words, will you make God capable of suffering? God though he was, he learned obedience in the school of suffering. God could know experimentally what suffering was only by taking a body. So the Blessed Mother is asked, "Will you make it possible for your creator to suffer?" Think of a mother, for example, who gives to a young son or daughter an automobile at the age of nineteen, which a short time afterward is the cause of a wreck and permanent injury. Would the mother ever forgive herself? And here Mary has to say yes, I will let him suffer.

A cross in the heart of God   *March 16*

The Father had a role in the Son's suffering. We can compare it to a father bringing a son to a dentist. The son has a bad tooth that is infected. That bad tooth causes a toxic condition in the son's body. The dentist says, "This infection is in the tooth. Your son will experience considerable pain. I may have to remove the tooth; I certainly will have to drill it, and then I shall have to remove that toxic condition." Now, the human race had a point of infection: our first parents. That sin created a toxic condition in the human race. When the drill is applied by the dentist, does the father say, "Do not do that; that hurts my son"? Or will the father deliberately allow his son to experience pain? Is there not a cross in the very heart of God?

The precious broken bottle   *March 17*

Our Lord attended a banquet in Bethany, given by Martha, Mary, and Lazarus. The twelve apostles were there. In the course of the dinner, Mary Magdalen—if she be Magdalen—took perhaps what was the fruit of an evil life, namely some precious perfume, to give it to the Lord. In those days, women often carried precious nard in a bottle about the neck. If one of their beloved ones died, they would break the bottle over the corpse and then sprinkle the corpse with perfume and throw the remains of the bottle on the corpse. Mary Magdalen came to the feet of our Lord, for in those days they reclined at table. She did not do what you and I would do. She did not pour out that precious perfume drop by drop as if to indicate by the slowness of the giving the generosity of the gift. She broke the vessel and gave everything, for love knows no limits. Immediately the house was filled with perfume. It was almost as if, after the death of that perfume and the breaking of the bottle, there was a resurrection. Broken things are precious. We eat broken bread because we share in the death of our Lord and his broken life. Broken flowers give perfume. Broken incense is used in adoration. A broken ship saved Paul and many other passengers on the way to Rome. Sometimes the only way the good Lord can get into some hearts is to break them.

A great sponge   *March 18*

Our Lord on the cross was very much like a great sponge that just wiped clean this earth and absorbed within himself all the sins of mankind, as if he himself was guilty. Dostoevsky, in the story of the underworld which told of his days of exile in Siberia, writes, "O God, could you not let me be a sponge to plug up some dirty old hole." Well, that was exactly what our Lord did for us. He was the great absorbent. That's where all our excuses ended. That's where our sins ended.

The Spirit and sin   *March 19*

The night of the Last Supper our Blessed Lord told of three effects of the Holy Spirit. One of them was: "He will convict you of sin, because you did not believe in me." How do we know we are sinners? By the Holy Spirit. Not because we break a law. There isn't a driver who hasn't broken the law against speeding. Did you ever lean over your steering wheel and say an act of contrition? Nobody is really sorry for breaking a law, unless he gets caught. The law is for the imperfect. Our Blessed Lord relates sin to unbelief—"Because you did not believe in me." If we did not believe in him, we crucified him. So what is sin? Sin is hurting someone you love. That is sin. That is why the crucifix reminds us of our sin. The life of each and every one of us has been written. The crucifix is my autobiography. The blood is the ink. The nails the pen. The skin the parchment. On every line of that body I can trace my life. In the crown of thorns I can read my pride. In the hands that are dug with nails, I can read avarice and greed. In flesh hanging from him like purple rags, I can read my lust. In feet that are fettered, I can find the times that I ran away and would not let him follow. Any sin that you can think of is written there. This is what the Spirit does for us.

From the cross our Lord looks down to his Blessed Mother
and St. John, and he develops this new relationship in the
kingdom of heaven. Now we've always thought, and rightly
so, of Christ the Son on the cross and the mother beneath
him. But that's not the complete picture. That's not the deep
understanding. Who is our Lord on the cross? He's the new
Adam. Where's the new Eve? At the foot of the cross. This
is not just Christ and his mother; it's the new Adam and the
new Eve. How did the old humanity begin? With the nuptials. How will the new humanity begin? With the nuptials.
If Eve became the mother of the living in the natural order,
is not this woman at the foot of the cross to become another
mother? And so the bridegroom looks down at the bride.
He looks at his beloved. Christ looks at his Church. There is
here the birth of the Church. As St. Augustine puts it, and
here I am quoting him verbatim, "The heavenly bridegroom left the heavenly chambers, with the presage of the
nuptials before him. He came to the marriage bed of the
cross, a bed not of pleasure, but of pain, united himself
with the woman, and consummated the union forever. As
it were, the blood and water that came from the side of Christ
was the spiritual seminal fluid." And so from this nuptials
"Woman, there's your son": the beginning of the Church.

Man and woman in the church   *March 21*

Our Blessed Lord said the word is the seed, the seed is the
word. Man gives the seed. The woman receives the seed,
fosters it, nourishes it, gives birth to it, loves it, trains it.
There's no such thing as inferiority or superiority. Instead of
being a question of inferiority and superiority, it is only a
question of the different roles that we play—the man is the

symbol of Christ, and the woman is the symbol of the Church. Many people no longer have an understanding of the Church as the body of Christ. Jesus loves his body. So when we forget the Church and begin to call her an institution, an establishment, the whole character of the nuptial bond is disrupted. The Blessed Mother beneath the cross is the symbol of the Church, and John is the firstborn. At Pentecost we find that the body has grown: here are 120, with the apostles, Mary in the midst of them.

We are all thieves   *March 22*

Crucified with Jesus were two thieves or revolutionaries. Why thieves? Because we are all thieves. We have all, as the prophet Malachi said, cheated God. We cheat him in our lives; we cheat him in our worship; we cheat him in our relationships with fellow man. So he is reputed with the wicked. And this is the symbol of the last judgment, because when the Lord comes on the last day, they will be separated and divided, the wheat and the tares, the sheep and the goats, the good fish and the bad.

The judgment of the thieves   *March 23*

Note that all are sinners, as the two revolutionaries, or thieves, were both sinners. They both blasphemed when they began. There was no difference between them. Then one of them responded to grace, and the other interpreted the power of God as doing something good for himself, and so he said, "If you're the Son of God, save yourself and save us." That's all God is for. What would he have done with his life had it been given to him? He would have gone on with the dirty business of thieving. So on the last day there will be the good and the bad. This is judgment in its prologue.

The two thieves judged themselves. The one asked to be taken down, the other asked to be taken up. There was something material in the soul of the one on the right that responded to that intercessory prayer of our Lord, "Father, forgive." Then there came the conviction of sin. This thief on the right said to his brother thief on the other side, "We are suffering justly for our sins. This man has done no wrong," And then he asked only to be remembered: "Remember me when you come into your kingdom." Kingdom? In the whole gospel is there any faith comparable to that of this man? Here he looks upon what is seemingly a condemned criminal— and so he spoke of him at the beginning—and he sees a crown of thorns as a royal diadem. The nail in his hand is a scepter. The blood is his royal purple. The crucifixion is his installation and coronation. And he asks to be remembered. The Lord replied, "This day thou shalt be with me in paradise." On the day we die we go to Christ. "This day thou shalt be with me in paradise." I always wonder why our Lord needed to say "in paradise", because to be with him is paradise. The thief died a thief, for he stole paradise. And paradise can be stolen again.

The tempters from the cross   *March 25*

Who were the tempters from the cross? Satan was the tempter at the beginning, telling Jesus how he could win the world without a cross, by allowing people to feed their own instincts, or by doing something spectacular like flying to the moon or jumping from a steeple. He also tempted Jesus to develop a theology which was increasingly important in his century, and destructive. This theology is politics. The world belongs to me, says Satan. So Satan was the first to tempt him from the cross. Then Peter tempted Jesus; that was why he was called Satan. And finally on the cross, the enemies came and said: Come down and we will believe. They would believe. But would they believe that he was the Son of God? Certainly. Believe that he founded a Church? Yes. Believe in the Eucharist? Yes. Only come down from that cross. That's all we ask. Come down and we would believe.

Centurion, come back   *March 26*

St. John, who stood at the cross and who understood the heart of Christ better than anyone else because he leaned against it at the Last Supper, said, "And all shall look on him whom they have pierced." And then at the end of his life, when he began to write the Book of Revelation, he describes Christ's coming again. "Behold he is coming with the clouds. Every eye shall see him. And among them, those who pierced him, and all the peoples of the world shall lament in remorse." We shall all see the heart of the Lord. As we review that love, we search for the centurion. Where is he? Centurion, come back. You have already acknowledged him as the Son of God, but come back. Come back even though his blood is at the end of your lance. Come back even though that sword fell and with one blow pierced two hearts: physically the heart of Christ, and mystically the heart of Mary. But one spear and two broken hearts for the world are broken bread. So centurion, come back. We want to tell you that there's another way to get closer to the heart of Christ than wounding him.

The cross and the anti-cross   *March 27*

Scripture never speaks of reconciliation except through the death of Christ. We are saved, in other words, by the cross

63

and Resurrection. It follows that the anti-cross is the sign of the demonic. It is interesting to discover how much the crucifix has been displaced or removed in schools in the last few years. I was in a retreat house giving a retreat. There were about 1,20 people there this particular night. I looked around for a crucifix. There was none. Upon enquiring, I found that there had not been a crucifix in that retreat house in the last seven years.

Peter and Judas   *March 28*

It is interesting to make a comparison between Peter and Judas. Our Lord warned both that they would fail. They both failed. They both denied or betrayed the Lord. They both repented. But the difference in the word *repent* is that Judas repented unto himself and Peter repented unto the Lord. They were the same up to that point. St. Paul, therefore, says there were two kinds of sorrow, the sorrow of the world and the sorrow of true faith. Judas no longer had any hope, having refused to return to the Savior. He took a rope and went out to some rocky ground, we know not where it was. He walked over the rocky ground, and those rocks seemed just as hard and cruel as his own heart, and the limb of every tree seemed like a pointing finger. Traitor, traitor, traitor. And the knot in every tree seemed like an accusing eye. And he hanged himself. And as the Acts of the Apostles tells us, "His bowels burst asunder." And he went to his own place. That is all.

The Agony in the Garden   *March 29*

When our Lord was in the garden, he was not suffering so much from pain as from evil. Remember that only the innocent know what sin is. We can become so feverish that we think that we are well. Only the sinless really know guilt. So our Lord now reaches back into the past, not thinking of the pains that he has endured since he put on this mortal frame, but he drags up to the present moment all the sins of the world. The sin of Adam; Cain was there, purple in the sheet of his brother's blood. The abominations of Sodom and Gomorrah were there. The coarseness of the Jews and the sometimes even greater coarseness of the Gentiles. All those sins and abominations and idolatries were there. And then with his infinite mind looking into the future, Jesus dragged back upon himself all of the sins that would ever be committed until the end of time. Sins that rent Christ's mystical body, sins of the old, who should have passed the age of sinning. Sins of the young, for whom the heart of Christ is tenderly pierced. Sins committed in the city, in the city's fetid atmosphere of sin. Sins committed in the country that made all nature blush. Sins too awful to be mentioned, sins too terrible to be named. And Samson-like Jesus reached up and pulled down this horrible edifice of sin upon himself until the blood began to pour out from his body forming on the olive roots, red drops, the first red beads in the rosary of redemption.

Filling up the quota   March 30

St. Paul, in his letter to the Colossians, a letter which he wrote from prison, said: "It is now my happiness to suffer for you. This is my way of helping to complete in my poor human nature the full tale of Christ's affliction still to be endured for the sake of his body, which is the church." Our Lord says, "It is finished." Paul says, "It is not finished." Certainly the sufferings of our Blessed Lord were finished in him as the head of the Church, but they are not finished in his body. The quota of the physical Christ is finished. The quota of the mystical Christ is not. So St. Paul says: I am helping to fill up that quota. And so Christ's wounds are eternally fresh. They're all over the world. They're in those who have the faith, and they're in those who do not have the faith. This vision will come to us as we live close to the cross and meditate on the Passion of our Lord. Nothing gives us so much understanding of the love of God, the sacrificial love, as God coming down to this world from heavenly head-quarters and saying, I will take the pain as my own. This vicarious love is the *agape* love of Christianity. No wonder, then, St. John tells us about the Lamb, the Lamb with the marks of slaughter upon him. If Christ is in agony until the end of the world, and he is, then our vision changes. The Passion is not a past history like the battle of Waterloo. So maybe we had better change our lives to be more closely linked with the Lamb who has the marks of slaughter upon him.

Mary and John   *March 31*

On the cross we no longer have Christ and his Mother, or Jesus and Mary. I know we speak of the sorrowful Mother at the foot of the cross, but I don't think she was sorrowful, I think she was suffering. I cannot imagine the mother of the Maccabees as being sorrowful when she sent her seven sons to death. There must have been a certain joy in the mother's heart as she gives her son. But there's something different here. At this moment on the cross we no longer have Jesus and Mary. We have the new Adam and the new Eve. Our Lord on the cross is the new Adam, the Blessed Mother at the foot of the cross is the new Eve. And we're going to have the consummation of a marriage, and out of the consum-mated marriage of the new Adam and the new Eve is going to begin the new Church of which John will be the symbol.

And so the new Adam looking down now to the woman, says: "Woman, your son." And to the son, he did not say "John" (he would have then been only the son of Zebedee), but "Son, your mother." Here is the begetting of a new life. The Blessed Mother becomes the symbol of the Church. And as Eve was the mother of the living, so Mary becomes the Mother of the new living in the order of grace.

April

Why all this waste?   *April 1*

After Mary broke the bottle of perfume, the odor filled the
house and Judas got one whiff of it. Oscar Wilde describes a
cynic as one who knows the price of everything and the
value of nothing. Judas immediately put a price on the perfume: 300 days' wages. It was very precious perfume. And he
interrupted this beautiful scene of the woman breaking her
precious bottle over the feet of our Lord, by challenging the
Savior. Judas said, "Why all this waste? It could have been
sold, given to the poor." Why all this waste? Why build beautiful cathedrals to adore the sovereign Lord of the universe?
Why all this waste? Why should young men and women
consecrate themselves wholly to the service of the Lord? Why
all this waste? Why should beauty be dedicated to him, and
not be profaned in the world? Why all this waste? And he
who said that was at that time stealing money from the apostolic purse. Our Blessed Lord did not let him escape with
that challenge; he said to Judas, "Judas, the poor you have
always with you. You do not always have me." If you are so
anxious about serving the poor, there are never occasions
that are wanting. But I am with you only for a short time.

Have you sold Christ?   *April 2*

Judas went to the Sanhedrin, to the chief council of the city,
and said to them, "What will you give me?" Everything wrong

begins with "Give me." The prodigal son when he left home said, "Give me." "What will you give me if I deliver him to you?" They talked among themselves, and they fixed the fee at the price of a slave. What was our Lord worth? About thirty pieces of silver. A slave, he was. The Greek word for "slave" is *doulos*. It is used over forty times in the New Testament. A slave does two things: he does hard things, and he does dirty things, even bearing the burden of human sin. So the price was fixed; they gathered together thirty pieces of silver, and they dropped them one by one into that hand that was blessed by the Lord when Judas was called to be an apostle. Judas went out with his thirty pieces of silver. Remember, you can sell the Lord, but you can never buy him. We get sick of selling the Lord as Judas was, when he brought back his money and flung it into their faces, saying "I've betrayed innocent blood." Think about your lives. How many times have you sold Christ?

A word for the haters   *April 3*

Our Lord spoke from the cross to those who hated, for there are an abundance in the world who cannot endure his name. They hurled a challenge to him. They said, "If you are the Son of God, come down from that cross." Come down and we'll believe. Sure, they will believe. They'll believe anything: just no cross, no mortification, no self-denial. This is not weakness to hang on the cross. This is obedience to the law of sacrifice. If he came down, he never would have saved us. It is human to come down. It is divine to hang there. So there are many who say, "I'll believe anything; I'll believe that he is divine; I'll believe in his Church; I'll believe in his pontiff, only no cross, no sacrifice." That's all. George Bernard Shaw said, "It's that that bars the way." Sure, it bars the way. It bars the way to hell. And for them our Blessed Lord merely prayed for forgiveness. He said, "Father, forgive them, they know not what they do." It is not wisdom that saves, it is ignorance. If we knew what we were doing when we crucified the Lord, we would never be saved. It is only in the ignorance of what we do when we crucify him that we come within the pale of hearing the cry, forgive.

A word for the atheists   *April 4*

On the cross our Lord spoke to the atheists, to the communists, to the agnostics, to the unbelievers, to the fallen-away, all of whom live an inner kind of hell—particularly those who have had the faith and lost it. Hell does not begin in the next world. It begins here. How will an atheist, an agnostic, or an infidel ever be saved, if the Lord on the cross does not take means to redeem them? So our Blessed Lord now undertakes to suffer that loneliness, isolation, and separation from God that all atheists feel. He permitted himself, therefore, to be without any divine consolation, to walk on the very brink of hell, to feel what it is to be damned. At that moment, when the sun hid its light, almost ashamed to shed its light on the crime of deicide, our Lord, now in that darkness of the very day, put on this darkness of soul and in reparation for all the atheists cried out, "My God, my God, why have you abandoned me?" That makes it possible for Brezhnev to save his soul: if Brezhnev hears that cry. The Lord felt the hell of Voltaire, of Camus, of Sartre, of Julian the Apostate, of all who deny their Lord. And from that day on, they need only cry to him to be saved. *But they must cry.*

What Christ did for us   *April 5*

I recall the legend of two brothers, one of whom was very good, while the other became very wicked. One day the wicked brother ran home and the robe that he wore was spotted with blood. He said, "I've just killed a man." And his brother said, "I will take your robe and you take mine. You leave." And the guilty brother left, the police came in, arrested the one who had on the robe filled with blood, and he was condemned to death. When he was dying, he sent a message to his brother. He said, "I'm sending you a white robe. Remember that I died to save you." Now that's precisely what our Lord did for us. He wore our robe of sin.

There is a man on the cross   *April 6*

Whenever there's silence round about me, by day or night, I am startled by a cry. It came from the cross the first time I heard it, and I went out and searched and found a man in the throes of crucifixion. I said, "I will take you down." He said, "I cannot be taken down until every man, woman, and child come together to take me down." "What can I do?" I said, "I cannot bear your cry." And he said, "Go into the world and tell everyone you meet there is a man on the cross."

Our Lord and pain   *April 7*

One of life's great scandals is pain, not only in ourselves, but in others. Pain will always be a trouble for the human mind as well as for the human body. How did our Lord look upon pain? When he went into the garden of Gethsemane on Holy Thursday night, there was an alternative presented to him: the alternative of the sword and the cup. Our Blessed Lord had before him, as it were, the cup of all the world's sin, which he would drink to its dregs in order that no other redeemer would be needed. As he abandoned himself to his Father's will, coming down on that moonlit night was a band of about two hundred, led by Judas. Peter took out a sword to defend Jesus. And our Lord said to Peter, "Put the sword back again into its scabbard. They who take the sword will perish by the sword. Shall I not drink the cup my Father gave?" My Father? Not Pilate, not Herod, not you and me, not the people? Is this the cup the loving Father gives? That's precisely the point. All pains, all trials of life, pass through God's hands first before they ever come to us. Before Satan could strike Job, God reviewed the punishments that Satan would visit upon Job and said, "You may touch everything except his soul." And so now our Blessed Lord is saying "The pains that we have are seen and known by the Father." That was the way he looked on pain.

His own received him not   *April 8*

When our Lord came to this earth, the gospel says of him, "He came unto his own and his own received him not." He had to be born under the floor of the earth, in a cave. One has to stoop to enter a cave. And the stoop is the stoop of humility. At the end of his life he was rejected by the earth again. The trees turned against him, the trees that he made, for they gave him a cross. The bowels of the earth turned against him, for they produced a hammer and nails. The roses blushed a deeper red, for from their branches came a crown of thorns. And the earth itself would not have his feet, so they raised him above it. As earth rejected him, so did the heavens. There was darkness over the earth for three hours. And the sun which he had made as a symbol of himself and as death and resurrection in daily life now hid its light, almost as if ashamed to shed itself upon the crime of deicide.

What it means to be a Christian

As the rich brother takes upon himself the debts of his bankrupt brother, so our Lord takes upon himself all the discord and disharmonies and all the sins and all the guilt of man as if he himself were guilty. As gold is sucked into the furnace to have its dross burned away, so God takes human nature, and plunges it into Calvary to have our sins burned away. Or to change the figure: since sin is in the blood, Jesus poured out his blood for redemption, for without the shedding of blood there is no remission of sins. And then on Easter Sunday he rises again with his glorified, sinless human nature. And this becomes the first note of the new creation, the beginning of the new symphony which will be played again and again by the divine conductor. How are the notes added? We are the other notes, if, like Mary, we really consent to be added to that first note. How do we become added? We become added by the sacrament of baptism by which each man dies to the old Adam and incorporates himself to the new Adam, Christ. All of these notes that are added to this first note constitute the new body of Christ and what is known as his mystical body, the Church. This is what it means to be a Christian.

Attested by his enemies

Early Saturday morning, therefore, the chief priests and the Pharisees broke the Sabbath and presented themselves to Pilate saying, "This deceiver while yet alive said 'I am to rise again after three days.' Give orders then that his tomb shall be securely guarded until the third day, or perhaps his disciples will come and steal him away. And they could then say to the people, he has risen from the dead. This last deceit would be more dangerous than the others." But Pilate was in no mood to see this group. He had made his own official investigation. Christ was dead. He would not submit to the absurdity of using Caesar's armies to guard a dead Jew. Pilate therefore said to them, "You have guards, away with you. Make it as secure as best you know how." There must be a seal, and the enemies would seal it. There must be a watch, and the enemies must keep it. The certificates of the death and Resurrection must be signed by the enemies themselves. The Gentiles were satisfied through nature that Christ was dead, and the Jews were satisfied through the law that he was dead. As the Gospel of Matthew puts it, "And they went and made the tomb secure, putting a seal on the stone and setting a guard over it." The king lay in state with his guard about him. And the most astounding fact about this spectacle of vigilance over the dead is that the enemies of Christ expected the Resurrection, but his friends did not. It was the believers who were the skeptics. It was the unbelievers who were credulous.

The apostles were skeptics   *April 11*

If the Resurrection was merely an illusion, the touching of the body of Christ, the putting the finger into the hand, the hand into the side, as Thomas did, would certainly have cured any such illusion. Furthermore, when our Lord appeared he ate food; they saw the food vanish. He took bread; they saw the bread break. On another occasion he gave them bread and fish, and they were satisfied of their hunger. This certainly does not happen when there is only a dream or an illusion. None of the apostles expected a Resurrection. They had to be convinced. They had to be convinced the hard way, as Thomas had to be convinced. Believe me, the skeptics of today cannot compare with the skeptics of those days, namely, the apostles. They were the doubters, and when they were convinced, they proved that they believed by having their throats cut for the cause of Christ.

Christ's death and Resurrection remake us   *April 12*

Our Lord is not primarily a teacher, he is a Savior. That's the meaning of the word "Jesus": he will save us from our sins. Suppose we took a chalice as an example of what he did for us. Suppose the chalice were taken from the altar and made into a beer mug and delivered over to unholy uses, its shape and contour completely changed. Then it was found. How could it ever be restored again to the altar? Well first of all, we would have to put it into a furnace, burn off the old shape and form, and hammer it again into the pattern of a chalice. Then we would bless it and restore it to the altar. That is what God did with the human nature. He took this chalice of humanity, threw it into the fires of Calvary, where he was scourged and beaten, and then he was restored to a new shape on Easter and became the new creation. This is what he did with the pattern of human nature.

How Thomas knew it was the Lord   *April 13*

Finally, Thomas saw the risen Lord. We are perhaps a little too critical of Thomas because he doubted. But there was something rather commendable about that man, because Thomas was not going to surrender himself to any king but Christ. He could be a teacher; he could be proclaimed as a king; he could be a wonder-worker; he could do anything. But there was one kind of love that Thomas knew to be the test, and that was the love that was victimal, the love that went to the death for another.

That is the way that Magdalen recognized Jesus too. "In the place where they crucified him there was a garden", says

St. John—a place where new life springs up. As Magdalen fell at his feet, through tear-dimmed eyes, she saw the two red marks of nails and knew that it was he. And when the Lord appeared to Thomas, he satisfied his demand for sacrificial love by saying: "Thomas, put your finger here into my hands and your hand here into my side. And be not incredulous but believing." Thomas had the test, the test of a Resurrection presence. Blessed are they who have not seen but believe.

Superstar or super scar?   *April 14*

We've almost gotten away from the concept of sacrificial love in our modern world. We succumb to Jesus Christ Superstar and rejoice and sing songs to someone attired in Reynolds Wrap, to make him forget that he's dying without a resurrection. So we teach our young that he's a superstar. Superstar! Who's a star? Someone who has a star over his dressing room door; the communications media are mad about him. Our Blessed Lord had no star over his dressing room door. He was driven out of a city, out to a garbage heap and there crucified. Thomas did not want this superstar, he said, "Unless I can put my finger into his hand and put my hand into his side I will not believe." I want a God who goes to death. "For greater love than this no man hath." What Thomas wanted was not Christ the superstar but a super scar.

Who will roll back the stone?   *April 15*

His friends did not believe in the death and Resurrection of our Blessed Lord. First of all, when the women went to the grave, they did not go to greet the risen Savior. They brought spices to anoint a dead body. Their problem was in moving back the stone. In front of this subterranean grave there was placed a great millstone, with a hole in the center through which a pole would be put to roll away the stone. That is why they asked, "Who shall roll back the stone for us in order that we may anoint the dead body?" When they told the disciples, Peter and John, that the tomb was empty and the Lord had risen, Peter said, "Woman's tale." So they did not believe. The disciples at Emmaus that Sunday afternoon did not believe. Peter and Andrew and James and John went back to the fishing business. They did not believe. It took considerable convincing, the appearances of our Blessed Lord, and, above all, the descent of the Holy Spirit on Pentecost to confirm the Resurrection.

A summary of our life   *April 16*

Have you ever noticed in the Apostles' Creed how quickly we pass over the earthly life of our Lord? Born, suffered under Pontius Pilate, was crucified, rose from the dead. We say nothing about the beatitudes, nothing about miracles. Just he was born, suffered, died, and rose again. Just those three. That's all there is in life. We're born; the earthly life is passed over, because all that matters concerning an earthly life is whether we are doing the will of God. And then, resurrection. First, we are born to Christ in baptism. Remember that our Lord was born into a sinful, sorrowful humanity. If we follow him as a rule of life, we are born into that kind of a world: the poor, the afflicted, the sick, the ignorant. That is why Jesus' birth was in a stable. He identified with the poor. Here is the second great commandment: love your neighbor. The fundamental reason for loving our neighbor is because we're born into the same humanity that our Lord was born into, and we must help redeem it. Second, he suffered and was crucified. We suffer. Our Lord said, "In this world you will have tribulation." We are given crosses. We bear the cross

78

for him and with him, recalling always what he did for us. And finally, he rose from the dead. Scripture says of our Blessed Lord, "having joy set before him, he endured the cross." That means that in any kind of trial which we have, there should be a hidden gladness. Why? Because we're assured of the resurrection. Even though God does send us some kind of trial, if we've borne his cross, we can be absolutely sure of the crown.

Suffering and joy   *April 17*

In the course of my life I have dealt with all kinds of people, with those who have been sinners and returned to the Lord and suffered much and had an indescribable joy. One of the most joyful figures I ever met in my life was a leper woman in Jamaica. She had lost her arms and half of her legs, but she was always smiling and happy and saying, "But there's going to be a resurrection, and I will then have a glorified body." That must be our attitude.

The judge and his son   *April 18*

Imagine a judge having before him his own son who committed murder. He killed a boy. Now there's no doubt whatever of the son's guilt. The father–judge, bound to execute justice, sentences his son to death. That is justice. Then he says to the son, "Now I will take your place, I will die for you." That would be mercy. But that is not the complete picture.

Suppose that at the moment the son was sentenced to death, the boy that the son had murdered walked in alive. The son would say, "How can you condemn me for murder? You said I killed this boy? You see, he's alive. I'm innocent, I should be free." That's precisely the condition that we are in. We were guilty of sin but our Lord rose from the dead, took our guilt upon himself, and washed it away. Now we can say, "See, he's alive, he's not dead. I'm free." So that's why he came.

A new birth   *April 19*

It is common for a creature in one stage of its existence to have a capacity for passing into a higher stage. But it is unusual for a creature to have a capacity which can be developed only by some agency outside of it and adapted to it. It is in this condition that man is born of his human parents. He is born with the capacity for life higher than that which he lives as an animal in this world. There is in him a capacity for becoming something different and higher. That capacity lies dormant and dead until the Holy Spirit comes and quickens it. The influence has to come from without. There must be the efficient touch of the Holy Spirit, the impartation of his life. The capacity to be a child of God is man's, but the development of this lies with God. We have to be quickened from without. We cannot give physical birth to ourselves, and we cannot give divine birth to ourselves.

Mass in a Chinese prison   *April 20*

A bishop was put into a communist prison in China. After beatings and persecution his weight fell to about ninety pounds. Covered with vermin, prison sores, wearing a black stocking cap and a black kimono, he was unable to walk by himself. He always had to be supported by two fellow prisoners. Providentially, however, he was the only one in prison that was ever given bread and wine. The communists did not know why they gave it to him, but at any rate he had it. If they knew that he was going to say Mass with the bread and wine, they certainly never would have given it to him. Mass in a gothic cathedral, with all the pomp and splendor of liturgy, could never equal the beauty of that Mass that was said by the bishop as he leaned against the prison wall, with the tray before him, as he moved his fingers, saying over the bread, "This is my Body", and over the wine, "This is my Blood", and then secretly passing out communion to those who shared his faith.

Example that overcomes the world   *April 21*

After the communist revolution in China, a bishop was put in the death march where later he perished. A communist colonel who was in charge of the march put a sack around his neck. It weighed about thirty pounds. It was so tied that the rope would gradually tighten as he marched; the sack would become heavier, and the bishop would eventually be choked to death. As the march began, a fellow prisoner who later told me the story, broke ranks, went up to the communist colonel, and shouted at him, "Don't do that! Look at the man!"

The communist colonel looked at him as if for the first time in his life he really saw suffering, and then he said to the one who interrupted him, "Get back in line, you dog!"

The death march began, and this friend of mine said that he tried to peer through the marching lines of the prisoners to see if he could catch a sight of the bishop, supported by two fellow prisoners. After about a mile he saw him. The bishop was still standing, but the sack was not on his back. The sack was on the back of the Communist colonel. I asked, "What happened?"

He said the Communist colonel put it on his own back And why? He said, "I think he was edified by the patience and resignation of the good bishop. In any case the communist was arrested for having done that service, and the last we heard he was in prison."

We belong to another world   *April 22*

Someone gave me a canary to be my companion during a long sickness. If I told that bird, "You are in this tiny, little cage and you have wings, but this is the right place for you", I'm sure the bird would be depressed. If, however, the bird could understand, and I said to him, "You're in the wrong place. You have a gift of song that should mount to the heavens, and you have wings that should fly", the bird would then be happier. So we are unhappy when we are locked in this little cosmos, which could be shattered by a bomb. But if we are told that there is another world, then life becomes a little bit happier.

God works in unseen ways   *April 23*

A man I evangelized some years ago, Louis Budenz, the former editor of the communist *Daily Worker*, died just a few years ago. I was talking to his widow on the phone the other day, and she recalled the first time that we met. Budenz, as the editor of the *Daily Worker*, wrote to me and said, "Will you have dinner with me?" It was rather embarrassing. I had been writing articles against the communists, and he had been writing in the *Daily Worker* against me. Not until after his death did I know that it was the head of the Russian Politburo who ordered Budenz to ask me to dinner. They felt that I was doing too much harm to the cause and, since he once had the faith as a boy, that he could approach me. But I didn't know that then.

As we sat down to table, Budenz said, "Now I will tell you what we communists have against you. You do not believe that Russia is a democracy."

"Well," I said, "how can it be a democracy in light of article 125 of your constitution?"

He said, "What is article 125?"

"Well," I said, "as you see, I know your constitution better than you do. So we're not going to talk about it—we're going to talk about your soul."

Much later I learned that when he went home that night, he said to his wife, "I was never so angry in my life. Here I was, sent by the Politburo to talk communism to this man who knows it, and after he mentioned article 125, he said, 'I am not interested in your communism, I want to talk to you about your soul.' Imagine, my soul. I'm not interested in that." And from that point on, she told me, that whenever I appeared on radio, he would become furious that my voice was heard in the house and order that the radio be turned off. But Mrs. Budenz also said, "I was not a Catholic; I was a communist. We were not married, just living together. But do you know that every night before we went to sleep, he would reach over and make the sign of the cross on my forehead. I never knew why he did that. I did not know what it was." Seven years later I received a letter from him asking to see me about his soul. And she asked him then, "Why are you writing to him when you hate him so much?"

He replied, "Because he talked to me about my soul. All this time I was worried, really troubled in spirit."

What do you deserve?   *April 24*

Look into your own heart. I've looked into mine. I've had a great deal of suffering in the eighty-three years of my life—physical suffering and other suffering. It should never have happened, and it has lasted for many years. Yet, as I look back, I know very well that I have never received the punishment that I deserved. God has been easy with me. He has not laid on me burdens that were equal to my failures. If we look into our own souls, I think that we will also come to the same conclusion, for God speaks to us in various ways. As C. S. Lewis put it, "God whispers to us in our pleasures, he speaks to us in our conscience, and he shouts to us in our pain." Pain is God's megaphone. And unlike the ripples that are made in a brook or that you see when you throw a stone in a pond, the ripples of pain, instead of going out to distant shores, narrow and narrow and come to a central point where there is less of the outside of the circle and more of the center. Not the ego, but the real person and the real self. And one begins to find oneself alone with God. That is what happens in pain.

Forming Christ in Russia   *April 25*

An archbishop friend of mine who speaks perfect Russian was in Russia not long ago. He wandered to a town in the southern part of the country and into a large church. The church was empty except for a coffin and three nuns on either side. Evidently they were praying for the person who was before them. The archbishop knew that someone had followed him. Afraid that he had been followed by a government agent, he decided not to talk to the sisters. They were dressed in a crazy-quilt combination of rags. Evidently they had collected thousands of pieces of different-colored cloth and made habits. They were recognizable, even in Russia.

In order to find out who had followed him the archbishop said to the man, "Someone dead, eh?"

The man said, "Yes, she's my sister."

So the archbishop then read a funeral service for her. Then this man brought him to a small walled yard at the edge of the city, where there was a hole in the lower part of the wall. He went in and talked to several sisters; he heard beautiful choral singing coming from another room. He said it was heavenly.

He asked one of the sisters, "Whose voices are these?"

She said, "These are our novices, our new vocations."

"May I see them?" he asked.

"No, no one may see them", replied the sister.

He said, "What is your purpose?" She said, "We live in a godless world and our purpose is to bring back Christ. The only way that we can ever bring him back is by imitating the Blessed Mother. People drop rags in that hole you saw in the wall and drop in pieces of food; that's how we live. Out of those rags we make a habit. And we have dedicated ourselves to the Blessed Mother who formed Christ in her body. We beg her every day to help form Christ in us, that he may once again return to our country."

Where has hell gone?   April 26

We used to believe that, as the Lord taught, there is a heaven for those who do good, a hell for those who do evil, and the earth, which is the place of probation. We finally denied heaven, hell, and earth all for various reasons. We said that they smacked of a universe that was not very scientific. But when we denied hell, it went somewhere else. Where did it go? It went on the inside of human hearts. Human hell, with all of its psychic madness, began to take over. We had to be relieved from these burning flames. Conscience has a thousand tongues, and each tongue brings in a different tale, and every tale condemns me as a villain. No wonder Macbeth asked about his wife, "Canst thou minister to a mind diseased, pluck from the memory a root of sorrow, raze out the rooted cobblets of the brain and by some sweet oblivious antidote cleanse the stuffed bosom of that perilous stuff that weighs upon the heart?" So that's why we had to seek all kinds of psychic relief and deadening of consciousness, because hell moved inside and finally we couldn't endure that hell. What have we done with hell in the last ten or fifteen years? We have made it into nuclear bombs. The movies become the interpreters so that catastrophes, judgments, towering infernos, wrecks, disasters, apocalyptic events, all of these terrible endings seize upon the mind to make it forget that brood of nocturnal serpents. They will not be still.

Thirst for holiness   *April 27*

There is a spiritual thirst, as we read in one of the psalms: "I thirst for the living God, when will I appear before him?" As he says "I thirst", our Lord is thirsting for return to his Father. The night before, at the Last Supper, he prayed to his Father and asked for the glory that was his before the foundations of the world were laid. He told his disciples that he was going to prepare a place for them. Now he has this thirst, to return again to his Father. Applying that spiritual thirst of our Lord to ourselves, what is it that we have if we love the Lord? We have a thirst for holiness. We want to be saints. We want to be happy, to be at peace on the inside, to be one with the Father. What is sanctity? Sanctity is Christ living in me so that his mind possesses my mind and I am governed by his truth. That's sanctity. He's in my will, and all things that are pleasing to him I do. He's in my body, so that my body becomes a tabernacle. Sanctity is not only Christ in me, it's making Christ known to others. It's being loveable. It's making Christ loveable. When others see us, they see Christ.

Judas and social justice   *April 28*

What our Lord said to Judas, he says to the world today:
You seemingly are very interested in social justice. Why are
you not concerned about individual justice? You love your
neighbor; why do you not love God? This is the attitude of
the world today. We have swung away from a period in
which we were concerned with individual sanctification to
the neglect of the social order. Now we have gone to the
extreme of being immersed with social justice, civil rights,
and so forth, and we are not the least bit concerned about
individual justice and the duty of paying honor and glory to
God. If you march with a banner, if you protest, then your
individual life may be impure, alcoholic, anything you please.
That does not matter. Judas is the patron saint of those who
divide that universal law of God: Love God and love
neighbor.

Reparation   *April 29*

We hardly think about reparation any more. We seem to have
dropped it in the Church. We have reparation in the human
body. When I had my open-heart surgery, I was bleeding to
death. I depended upon eighty people who gave me eighty
pints of blood. The human body has only eight pints. Vol-
unteers had to supply eighty pints to keep me alive. They
were filling up the quota of my life. And just as we have a
kidney transplant, even a heart transplant, so we have the
transplanting of merits, of prayers, and sacrifices from one
member of the Church to the other, to cure those members
of their anemic condition. We're living in a decade that needs
reparation more than any other decade in the past one hundred years. But we're failing to find it.

I was talking to a young woman who was in an iron lung for twenty-one years. The only part of her body that she could move was her head. She told me that she was visited the week before by six seminarians. They told her they were about to be ordained priests. She told them, "I hope you're also going to be ordained victims. Because our Lord was not only a priest, he was a victim; he offered himself for others. So you have to do that." They replied that the Lord didn't want them to suffer. She said, "You young men are imposing a tremendous additional penance on me to make you worthy of your priesthood." She was filling up in her own body the sufferings that were wanting to them. So those of us who have the faith have to begin restoring the idea of reparation.

May

Two hundred men and one woman   *May 1*

I once gave a retreat to the monks of Gethsemane in Kentucky. At that time there were well over two hundred of them in the monastery. At the end of compline, when the chapel was in total darkness, they began the "Salve Regina". Way at the far end of this great chapel there was a large window. As a faint light began to play on it, it turned out to be an image of the Blessed Mother, surrounded by saints. And as they sang, more and more light poured upon it, until she almost seemed alive. I have never seen so many men in love with one woman. It would positively tear your heart out as they sang to the glory of the woman that they loved. It was a happy memory, this singing.

The wedding feast at Cana   *May 2*

Picture the marriage feast of Cana. There our Blessed Lord is beyond the Jordan, gathering up his first disciples. Mary is already at the feast. The Lord comes with his new disciples, and Mary, who always knows our wants before we know them, says, "They have no wine." They had water, the water of the Old Testament, but they had no wine. And Jesus replies, "Woman"—not mother—"Woman, what to me is to thee?" That is the way it is in the original. "My hour has not yet come." The hour refers to his Passion and death, his combat with evil. Now he is equivalently saying to his Mother,

"My dear Mother, you want me to begin my public life, to declare myself the Messiah and the Son of God. Do you realize that the moment I do that, your relationship to me changes? You will then no longer be my Mother. You will then be the Mother of everyone whom I will redeem. You will be the universal Mother of all mankind. You will be the woman of Genesis. You will be the Mother of the living." Mary's heart must have burned at not hearing herself called "Mother". So our Blessed Lord, it seems, anticipated his public life. It is not often that mothers send their sons to the battlefield. Mary did. If the Father sent the Son, the Mother would send the Son.

Who is my mother?   *May 3*

Our Lord did his first miracle at the request of his Mother. A short time later, the Mother, fearful of the exhaustion of preaching during the day and praying on the mountaintop at night, sent a message to him. When the messenger announced, "Your mother is here", he turned to the crowd and said, "Who is my mother? Who is she?" What would our mothers say if we said that? "Who is my mother?" He is reminding her that in the kingdom of heaven there are no more ties of flesh and blood. The only bond that exists in the kingdom of heaven is the spiritual bond of obedience to the Father's will. So that the seeming rebuke turns into the greatest of compliments. "He that does the will of my Father in heaven is my mother." And who ever obeyed the will of the Father in heaven as closely as Mary?

The liberated woman   *May 4*

How did our theologians ever get the notion that the Vatican Council did away with devotion to our Lady? Was it because we didn't make a separate treatise? As a matter of fact, she was included in the treatise on the Church as Mother of the Church. She is the Mother of the Church, and our Mother. And she had an hour on the night of the Last Supper, when there was a mutual sorrow in the hearts of the disciples and our Blessed Lord. Our Lord used two feminine examples to explain sorrow. One was the hen that gathers chickens under her wings, and the other was the woman. He said, "When the woman is in labor she is in anguish because her hour has come, but she rejoices when the son is born." In the original it is not when *a* woman's hour has come, it is when *the* woman's hour has come. Our Lord had his hour, the Blessed Mother had her hour. And they both have their day. He rose from the dead; she was assumed into heaven. There's a woman in heaven. We can teach the world about woman's liberation. We have got the only liberated woman in all history. So if he had his hour, in reparation for sin, if Mary had her hour, then we can have ours.

The virgin birth of the Church   *May 5*

The virgin birth of Christ became the virgin birth of the Church. Here we pass from the Incarnation to the crucifixion. Remember that our Blessed Lord changed his attitude toward his mother at the marriage feast of Cana. She was then known as the Mother of Jesus. But at the marriage feast of Cana he called her "woman". Going back to Genesis, this is the woman whose seed would crush the head of the serpent. Then a year and a half later, when she was worried about him, and sent messages to him, imagine him saying, "Who is my mother?" He took all relationships out of the order of blood. For Christ they no longer exist. "He who does the will of my Father is my mother, my brother, my sister."

A woman clothed with the sun   *May 6*

The Church then has had a virgin birth. As we lose our
respect for the virgin birth of Christ, we lose our respect for
the virgin birth of the Church. We no longer understand
her as the bride of Christ. When we get to heaven, in what
celebration are we going to assist? Nuptials: the marriage of
the Lamb. In the twelfth chapter of the book of Revelation
we have another image of the Blessed Mother in the con-
stant struggle of the Church, or the bride, with the devil.
"And there appeared a great portent in heaven, a woman
robed with the sun, beneath her feet the moon and on her
head a crown of twelve stars. She was pregnant and in the
anguish of her labor she cried out to be delivered." The
original Greek is in the present tense. Even in the book of
Revelation the Blessed Mother is always bringing forth
children. That's the Church.

A word for the suffering   *May 7*

Not only are there those who lead evil lives and suffer, but
there are also those who lead good lives and suffer. At the
foot of the cross there are good lives, the best of lives—
particularly that of the Blessed Mother. We sometimes ask,
"Well, why should I suffer? What evil have I ever done?"
What evil did Mary ever do? What evil did our Lord do?
Remember that we are called to share in the redemption of
our Lord. As St. Paul says, "I fill up in my flesh the sufferings
that are wanting to the passion of Christ." Didn't Christ
suffer enough? Yes. But for whose sake? For the sake of his
body, which is the Church. As the centuries go on, we continue the redemption of our Lord. Our Mary was summoned at the very moment of his birth to share in his
sufferings. When she brought the divine child to Simeon,

Simeon said, "A sword shall pierce your heart too." You brought your child into the world without pain, but everyone else in this world who becomes a brother of Christ and a child of Mary causes agony to that Mother. And our Blessed Mother shared secondarily in the redemption of our Blessed Lord by bearing us, her children, spiritually. That is why we can call her Mother.

Liberation   *May 8*

Mary could teach us about liberation. Liberation is not only from something, it's *for* something. There was another woman who lived at the same time as the Blessed Mother who believed in the wrong kind of liberation, and that was Herodias. She believed first of all in liberation from a husband, so she could have as many men as she wanted. Second, she didn't believe in moral training for her children, for she taught her daughter to be a temptress. And third she hated religion, because she beheaded John the Baptist. Now that's not the kind of liberation that our Blessed Mother stood for.

Life and justice   *May 9*

What was the liberation Mary stood for? First of all, she stood for life. Here was a young woman who was so poor she had nothing but doves to offer at the temple. There was no housing, so for childbirth she had to go to a stable. There's the shame associated with a virgin bearing a child. And with all of that poverty and all of that shame, should she have aborted? No, she believed in liberation for life. She also believed in liberation for justice. What greater declaration of justice is there than the *Magnificat* of Mary. Speaking of exalting the poor, and exalting the humble, this is the liberation of justice.

Equity

Mary stands for the liberation of equity. She goes beyond equality and stands for equity. Equity handles all the cases that are beyond justice. Men have handled a just world and not handled it too well. There was a statue in Chartres of Our Lady of Equity. On either side of the cathedral of Chartres were great windows, one series of windows donated by the family of Pierre de Durre, and one series donated by Blanche of Castile. They were rival families, and in the center sat the Lady of Equity, reconciling the families. This is liberation.

What is the ascension?

We are not to think of the ascension as a locomotion. We are not to think of our Blessed Lord, for example, as going beyond the farthest star, or to think of him as being so many millions of light years away. Nor are we to think of him as going up from one point to another. Certainly we are not to envisage the ascension as a form of space travel. Our Blessed Lord once had a descent, that is to say that he came down from heaven, but that really did not mean a physical descent. It was, rather, a drawing aside of the veil in which divinity was revealed to humanity. So, too, the ascension is not like a rocket. Our Lord is no closer to heaven if we imagine him passing the star Arcturus. Rather the ascent and the descent that are mentioned in the Creed and in Christian doctrine refer to humiliation and exaltation. When Jesus came to this earth, he humbled himself. When he ascended into heaven, he was exalted.

What does the word "seated" mean, when we say, "He is seated at the right hand of God, the Father Almighty"? The word "seated" here means repose after conflict. The cross was left behind, all of its dust and thirst and struggle and pain. Being seated does not mean that our Lord is passive. You remember in the book of Genesis that God was said to have rested after creation. Does that mean he was tired? Certainly it did not imply that his creative arm was weary. Our Blessed Lord sits not to recuperate, but because his work is done. On the cross Jesus said, "It is finished." All the types and figures and symbols of the Old Testament had now been completed. Every word of scripture had been fulfilled. There is no other mediator. The cross is the perpetual atonement and satisfaction for the sins of men. As our Lord said, praying to his heavenly Father, "I have finished the work that thou hast given me to do." That is the meaning of our Lord being seated.

Entering beyond the veil   *May 13*

The ascension of our Lord is described as a high priest entering the sanctuary beyond the veil. What does this expression mean? It refers to something in the Old Testament. The temple of Jerusalem and the tabernacle in the desert before it, had a veil hanging before the holy of holies. The veil was very heavy, gorgeous, and mysterious. Behind that veil lay enshrined the symbols of Jewish history and Jewish faith. Behind it was the holy of holies. The priest was allowed to enter that holy of holies only once a year, and then only after he had purified himself with blood and sprinkled this veil with blood. When this happened, the people had for one brief moment some communication, thanks to their priests, with this holy of holies. But for the rest of the year it was hidden. What must the Jews have said to themselves as they looked at that veil? They knew they could not enter it. They must have said, "We are cut off from God." And that sentiment must have continued in the heart of every true man of the Old Testament. Now the veil in the New Testament is the flesh of our Lord. When he died on the cross, that veil of the temple was torn asunder. It was torn from top to bottom as if to indicate that it was not done in any way by the hand of man. In other words, this barrier between heaven and earth, between God and man is now destroyed. Thanks to the death of Christ, there is access to heaven, access to the heavenly Father. There might have been, indeed, some symbolism to the fact that the centurion pierced the side of our Blessed Lord, for as I said, sacred scripture calls his flesh the veil. And when Jesus' side was pierced, there was indeed revealed the holy of holies, which was the heart of the all-loving God.

He is our hope   *May 14*

Sinful humanity before the redemption could never enter behind the veil. Christ took upon himself our human nature; he bore it; he lived it; he died it. And he resumed it after he had laid it down. He glorified it, and he broke down that middle wall of partition between God and man, and thus he made peace. I look down to my nature laden with sin, and I despair. I look up to Christ's nature: it is now risen and ascended, and I'm full of joy. I look to my own nature, and I see my helplessness. I look up to Christ's nature, and I see my hope. I look down to my nature and see my sin. I look up to his, and I see his holiness. It is that holiness in the human nature of Christ that is risen now to heaven.

The ascension means we have a high priest in heaven who can sympathize with our weaknesses because he once bore our human lot. First, we say that there's a human nature in heaven. When God came to this earth, he took upon himself a human nature. That human nature was thrown into the pyres of Calvary in reparation for the sins of man; it rose and now ascends. There is a continuity between the Incarnation and the ascension. In the Incarnation our Lord took a body, yes, but not just a body to suffer. Otherwise he would have taken it for only a time. If he took that human nature just in order to suffer for our sakes, why did he not divest himself of that human nature? After all, his garments had been soiled and stained. They had borne the heat and burdens of the day. Why not throw them off? Christ's human nature was taken not just to atone for our sins. The end and purpose of God coming to earth was to bring us to perfect union with the Father. How could he do this? He could do it by showing that our flesh is not a barrier to that intimacy, by taking it up to heaven itself, and by showing that those who pass through trials and suffering in this life will have their body glorified. By sharing in Christ's cross we share in his glory. The goal of all humanity is in some way reached in the ascension.

We are in heaven already   *May 16*

When our Lord was talking to Caiaphas, he told him that one day he would see the Son of Man seated on the right hand of power. In other words, that human nature that was so humiliated is no longer a humiliated human nature. It is now glorified. His ascension is the true carrying of that real humanity, complete in all its parts, body and soul, up to the very throne of God. That is the purpose of the Incarnation: to be our model, to be our pattern. In a certain sense, because Jesus is the new Adam in heaven, you and I are there also. We are not yet there actually, but we are there potentially so long as we remain in a state of grace on this earth.

Like us in all but sin   *May 17*

Our Lord took a human nature in order that he might be able to sympathize with our weaknesses. The epistle to the Hebrews contains a beautiful text on this point. It reads, "It is not as if our high priest was incapable of feeling for us in our humiliations. He has been brought through every trial, fashioned as we are, only sinless." Our Blessed Lord in heaven is our high priest. He is our mediator. He is one who can understand us. He is not apart from us, because he had our human nature. That human nature, when it was on this earth, was so sensitive that it was thrilled by the beauty of a lily. It was moved by the fall of a wounded sparrow. It was keenly touched by anything that could touch a human heart, whether high or low, good or bad, friend or enemy. No man can be beyond the reach of that all-comprehending sympathy, because no man can ever be beyond the embrace of that love. Jesus can sympathize with the poor, because he was poor; with the weary and heavy-laden, because he has been tired and worn; with the lonely and misrepresented and persecuted, simply because he has been in that position. He can sympathize because he was tried, in mind as well as in heart, tried by fear, by sad surprise, by mental perplexity, and by the hard conflict with evil. He is able to feel to the uttermost for the keenest sorrows of our earthly lot. The beauty of it all is that this tried one is without sin. That is what enabled him to drink in sympathy, and nothing but sympathy in all sorrow, simply because he was without sin.

Christies our mediator   *May 18*

Now that Christ is in glory at the right hand of the Father,
what does he do there? Has he a work? Certainly: he's a
mediator. We might almost say that he's constantly showing
his scars to his heavenly Father and he is saying, "See these,
I was wounded in the house of those that love me. I love
men. I suffered for them. Forgive them, heavenly Father."
He is our sacrifice. He is ever-present before the Father. As
scripture puts it, "ever making intercession for us". You see,
we very often get a wrong understanding of the life of our
Lord. We think of him as just living on this earth, preaching
the beatitudes and suffering. No, Jesus did not come down
just for that. He is living, making intercession for us, the
representative of all who invoke him. Certainly he has finished the work of justice on earth because he paid the debt
of sin. But the work of mercy in heaven is unfinished. That
goes on and on. The reason it goes on is because we need his
intercession.

Christ revealed the Father   *May 19*

When our Lord was on this earth, he revealed the heavenly
Father. It was only through him that we knew how much
love the Father has for us. The Father so loved the world
that he sent his only begotten Son to save it. The night of
the Last Supper, Philip said to Jesus, "Show us the Father."
Our Lord replied, "Philip, have I been with you all this time
and still you do not understand the Father and I are one?" It
was the Father's love that sent the Son, so that our Lord was
a kind of a prism. Just as when the earthly sun shines through
a prism and splits the light into the seven rays of the spec-
trum, so too our Lord reveals the full love and goodness of
the heavenly Father.

The Holy Spirit reveals the Son   *May 20*

Just as the Son revealed the Father, so the Holy Spirit reveals
him. These are the words of our Lord, "And he will bring
honor to me because it is from me that he will derive what
he makes plain to you, because all that belongs to the Father
belongs to me." In these words our Blessed Lord is saying
that once he ascends to the Father, then all of the spiritual
blessings won by him on Calvary will be conveyed to us by
the Holy Spirit. Jesus said during his earthly life that we would
not understand his life, we would not receive all of the merits of his life until the Spirit came to this earth. The great
business of the Holy Spirit, therefore, is to stand behind the
scenes to make Christ more real. That is why the apostles
did not understand the crucifixion until after Pentecost.
St. Paul goes so far as to say that no one can call Jesus "Lord"
except by the Spirit. Oh, sure, you can pronounce the word
Jesus, but you do not know that Jesus is the Christ, the Son
of God, the Savior of the world, the Lord of the universe,
except by the Holy Spirit.

Our Comforter   *May 21*

As the telescope reveals not itself, but the stars beyond, so
the Holy Spirit reveals not himself, but Christ. Just think
how we are able in this age of ours to communicate with
distant parts of the earth thanks to electric or light waves.
Why, therefore, cannot our Lord, who dwells in heaven, be
within whispering distance of us, through his Holy Spirit?
Our Lord said to his apostles, "It is only for a short time that
I am with you, my children. I will not leave you orphans."
Then he promised his Spirit that would abide with them
forever. That Spirit he sent was to be another Comforter.
He was their Comforter on earth. And now his Spirit would

be their comfort, their Paraclete, their Advocate. Listen to the words of our Lord, "I will ask the Father and he will give you another Comforter, one who will dwell with you forever."

The Spirit makes Christ real   *May 22*

When our Lord was manifested to us, he spoke to us from without, but the Holy Spirit will speak to us from within. Does that mean that the Holy Spirit is to be a substitute for Christ? No. The Holy Spirit will make Christ more real than ever. Hear the words of our Lord, "And that day you shall know that I am in the Father, and you in me, and I in you." How would he be in us? By revealing his hidden excellence in our hearts. That is why St. Paul said that if we have known Christ according to the flesh, we know him so no longer. Because now we know him in another way. We know him through the Holy Spirit. Therefore the Holy Spirit, as our Lord said, will bear witness to him, not to himself.

We know Christ by the Spirit   *May 23*

You will often hear people say, "Oh, Jesus was a great teacher. Really, he and Lincoln and Plato have done a great deal for the world. If we wanted to solve all of our economic and social problems, all we would have to do is read the beatitudes of Jesus." People who talk that way do not understand that Jesus is the Christ, the Son of God, the Redeemer of the world. For them, Jesus is just another man. Why do they not know him? Because they do not have the Spirit. And why do they not have the Spirit? Because they have not obeyed the law of God, however little or however much they knew of it. Our Lord said, "If you love me, keep my commandments." Then the Holy Spirit will manifest himself to us. The purpose of the Holy Spirit is that of an artist. He draws a picture of our Lord on the canvas. He makes him real to us so that we understand. Just as the artist stays outside of the canvas, so the Holy Spirit is staying outside of the Christ whom he reveals to us.

Putting on Christ   *May 24*

To be filled with the Spirit is to be filled with Christ, so when we put on the mind of Christ, we put on the will of Christ. There's nothing in the gospels that gives us an answer to many of the problems of life and the difficulties of the day. If we were just simply to imitate the life of our Blessed Lord as is found in the gospels, we would all have to become carpenters. How, then, do we know what to do? The Spirit of Christ shows us what we are to do in each and every circumstance: the proper words to say, the right action, the kind of charity to perform. Now this Spirit of Christ that is in our soul manifests Christ to us. St. Paul uses the example of the human mind to make clear the Holy Spirit. He asks, "How do we know the thoughts of another person?" Well, it's because we have a soul and a spirit just as he has. Engineers understand engineers, and brokers understand brokers, and students at college understand students at the same college. Why? Because they all have the same spirit. They are human to begin with, and then they have the spirit of engineers and brokers and so forth. But why are we able to understand Christ? Because we have the Spirit of Christ.

Only by the Spirit can we learn Christ   *May 25*

The natural spirit, the purely human spirit, the spirit that is not yet holy cannot grasp the deep meaning of Christ. It is almost like expecting a canary in a cage to learn Shakespeare. He cannot do so. You would have to put your own brain inside of the canary's brain. So the brain of a scientist or dramatist cannot understand the mysteries of redemption because it lacks the Spirit. As St. Paul puts it, "The natural man receiveth not the things of the Spirit of God, for they are foolishness unto him. And neither can he know them because they are spiritually discerned." Trying to teach people about Christ and the mysteries of our holy faith is almost like trying to teach a blind man color, unless those people are ready to receive the Spirit of Christ himself. Now converts who take instruction come to know that Jesus is the Lord. Where do they learn it? From the Spirit. One becomes interested in the Church simply because he received a grace that illumined his mind and strengthened his will. The Holy Spirit does that. The Holy Spirit woos the soul, draws it into closer fellowship, to more intimate union.

The Holy Spirit and sin   *May 26*

The night of the Last Supper our Lord said that the Holy Spirit would convict us of sin. "The Spirit will come," Jesus said, "and it will be for him to prove the world wrong about sin. They have not found belief in me." When do we come to a real understanding of sin? Our Lord tells us that we understand through the Holy Spirit. No one who thinks it is just the breaking of a law really grasps the evil of sin. When we have the Spirit of Christ, we understand that sin is doing harm to one we love. That is why the crucifixion is the manifestation of sin. And that, as our Lord said, is unbelief in its essence—the absolute refusal to have the love and the blessings of God. The Holy Spirit reveals to us that sin is the refusal to accept the deliverance purchased by Christ. Nothing but the Spirit can really convince us of sin. How often, for example, is our conscience smothered by repeated evil

actions? We rationalize our evil deeds. Public opinion sometimes even approves of sin. But the Spirit reveals to us that all
unbelief is sin, that sin in some way is tied up with the
crucifixion.

The Spirit not the law   *May 27*

Every sinner who has the Spirit of Christ always thinks of
sin in relation to the crucifixion. That is when our Blessed
Lord becomes our hope. So there is nothing like the enlightened conscience, in which we are not under a law. Those
who really love Christ are beyond it. The Holy Spirit gives
us a sense of holiness, and holiness is separation from the
world. St. Paul says that his conscience was enlightened by
the Holy Spirit. Whenever, therefore, we do wrong, it is not
the law, it is not the commandments, it is the Spirit that tells
us that we are breaking off the relationship with love. That is
why St. Paul tells us that as often as we sin, we crucify Christ
anew in our hearts. Therefore the life of a true Christian is
not so much concerned with the avoidance of sin. We are
beyond that. Rather, it is an attempt to reproduce in ourselves the life of Christ. As our Lord said of his heavenly
Father, "All things that are pleasing to him, that I do." So we
say to the Trinity, "All things that are pleasing to God, that
we do." That constitutes our attitude toward sins, and it is
done through the inspiration of the Holy Spirit.

The Spirit is power   *May 28*

What therefore will the practical result of understanding the
Holy Spirit be? As you pray to the Holy Spirit to know Christ
and the fullness of his gospel and the love of the Father, you
will understand that he, the Holy Spirit, is the source of
power. Our Lord said, "I will send you power from on high."

Every day of my priestly life I pray for that power of the Holy Spirit: the power that is not human, the power that is not physical, the power that is not intellectual, but rather a power that comes solely from living the Christ life: power to influence people, the power to impress those who listen to me.

The role of confirmation   *May 29*

In confirmation, we are brought into God's spiritual army and into the lay priesthood of believers. Confirmation, like any other sacrament, is modeled upon the life of our Lord. Jesus had a double priestly anointing, corresponding to two aspects of his life. First was the Incarnation; that made him capable of being a victim for our sins. Because in the Incarnation he took upon himself a body, the human nature with which he could suffer, and therefore redeem us from our sins. As God, he could not suffer, but as man he could. This first aspect of the life of our Blessed Lord culminated in his Passion and death and Resurrection. Now there was another aspect of his life, a second anointing as it were, and that was the coming of the Holy Spirit in the Jordan. That ordained him for the mission of preaching the apostolate, and this reached its culmination, as far as the Church was concerned, in Pentecost.

Christ and the Spirit   *May 30*

The descent of the Holy Spirit on our Lord in the Jordan had a double effect. First, it prepared him for combat, for battle. This is what the gospel states: "Jesus returned from the Jordan full of the Holy Spirit and by the Spirit he was led out into the wilderness where he remained forty days, tempted by the devil." Just as soon as he received the Holy Spirit, he entered into the battlefield, into the conflict with Satan, who offered him the three easy ways from the cross. The Holy Spirit did something else. The Spirit not only prepared Jesus for combat, but also prepared him for preaching the kingdom of God. When our Lord, therefore, appeared at Nazareth, he said, "The Spirit of the Lord is upon me; he has anointed me, sent me out to preach the gospel to the poor, to restore the broken-hearted, to bid the prisoners go free, and the blind to have sight, to set the oppressed at liberty, to proclaim a year when men find acceptance in the Lord." Now after our Lord had received the Spirit and fulfilled these two missions, he instituted a sacrament, the sacrament of confirmation, by which this power and energy and strength of being a soldier of Christ and witness to Christ and the kingdom of God passes into our souls.

The Holy Spirit in the Trinity   *May 31*

The Father loves the Son and the Son loves the Father. Love is not in one alone; love is not in the other. The love that we have for one another is not just in me and not just in you. Love is always a bond between two or among several. That is why even lovers will speak of *our* love, something outside of the lovers themselves. So love is not in the Father, love is not in the Son, love is the mysterious bond uniting both. Because we are here dealing with the infinite, that divine love is so deep, so profound that it cannot express itself by canticles, words, or embraces. It can express itself only by that which signifies the fullness and exhaustion of all giving, namely, a sigh. Something that's too deep for words. That is why the bond of love between the Father and the Son is called the Holy Breath, the Holy Spirit. As the three angles of the triangle do not make three triangles, but one, so there are three persons or three relationships in God, but only one God.

June

The Holy Spirit and the Incarnation

The Father sent his Son. The Holy Spirit, however, is not apart from the mission of Incarnation. There are three distinct moments when, in relation to the humanity of our Lord, there was a special influx, an outpouring of the Holy Spirit. The first moment was at the Incarnation itself. To have generation, you have to have love, and here the love was not supplied by a human person, it was supplied by God himself. That breath of God, that *ruah* that brooded over creation, brooded over Mary for the new creation, and God became man. Then there came a second growing and increase in the Spirit. He was led by the Spirit into the desert to combat the evil spirit. A new Spirit, as it were, or rather a new power is needed now for the conflict with evil. God the Father speaks, and the Spirit appears under the form of a dove. In the Middle Ages, people used to say that the dove had no gall. That was why it was the symbol of the Spirit; there was no bitterness in it. The point is that our Blessed Lord did receive the Spirit in his humanity at the River Jordan. The third time was at his exaltation. We could pick out various passages in sacred scripture that show that he died for our sins with the Spirit; he rose from the dead with the Spirit; he became Lord of all things in heaven by the Spirit.

The Spirit in the Church June 2

There was no reference at the Vatican Council to the expression of Bossuet, "The Church is the prolongation of the Incarnation." Why did the bishops not use that expression? Because there had been a neglect of the Holy Spirit in our understanding of the Church. It is because the Holy Spirit, as it was important in the physical body of Christ, is also important in his ecclesial body. The Church, therefore, is the historical manifestation of the suprahistorical Christ, thanks to his Spirit. That's the Church. That is why we obey the Church: she is Christ, and the Spirit is in her.

A supernatural gift June 3

It is important to know that the gift of the Holy Spirit is first of all that which vivifies the Church, and it affects her members by making us the adopted children of God. That's the gift of God. That is grace. It is a supernatural gift. For example, if a marble floor would suddenly begin to bloom, that would be an act which does not belong to the potencies and powers of a marble floor. Therefore, it would be supernatural, if the flowers on the altar suddenly began to move from the shade and into the sunshine, that would be a supernatural act for flowers. If while I was talking a dog came in and said to me, "Why didn't you quote 2 Corinthians when you were talking about the Holy Spirit?" that would be a supernatural act for a dog. Likewise, the privilege of being just creatures of God and partakers of his divine nature no more belongs to us than blooming belongs to marble, or locomotion to a flower, or speech belongs to a dog. It is a gift. We are all receivers. The important mission of the Spirit is to make us like Christ.

Why Jesus left us   *June 4*

There resides in us the raw material for living with and by
the Spirit of God. Why didn't our Lord remain on earth?
There could have been many advantages. We could have been
thrilled by the majesty of his bearing, awed by his presence
and his words. Yet he said: "It is better for you that I go. For
if I go not, the Spirit will not come to you"—the Holy Spirit.
The Spirit will not come. If Jesus had remained on earth, he
would always be outside of us, like an example to be copied,
like a model outside of an artist. If he left and sent his Spirit,
then he would be a veritable life to be lived. So Christ sends
his Spirit to us.

Christ, the Spirit, the Church   *June 5*

Who reveals Christ? He's hiding behind something: the Holy
Spirit. For on the night of the Last Supper our Lord said,
"He will glorify me; he will reveal me." That's how we know
Christ, not just by studying the "motions of credibility":
prophecies and miracles and "the consonance of right reason
with the aspirations of the heart", as Vatican I put it. We
know Christ through the Spirit. That is why Paul said that
only through the Spirit can we call Jesus Lord. Therefore,
through the increase of the Spirit, we deepen our knowledge of the Lord. Who reveals the Spirit? The Church. Too
often when people think of the Spirit, they always begin
with Pentecost. That was not the beginning of the life of the
Spirit. After the Resurrection, our Blessed Lord breathed
upon his apostles. "Receive ye the Holy Spirit; whose sins
you shall forgive they are forgiven." First to his Church:
this is the beginning of the outpouring of the Spirit. Then
at Pentecost there comes another. But see how the Church
has grown by this time. The Blessed Mother in the center,

the apostles, and then the 120 others. But it is therefore the Spirit that gradually unfolds itself in the Church. That is how we come to a theological knowledge of the three Persons. When we detach the Spirit from the Church, we are apt to go awry.

The Spirit unifies our lives   *June 6*

What does the Spirit do to us? It unifies our lives. The Spirit takes possession of the intellect so that we possess the truth of Christ, of the will, so that we have his power, which is grace, and of the body so that it becomes the temple of God. It unifies all our activity. Without the Spirit, we are disjointed, disunited. The best psychological explanation of man that was ever given is in the seventh chapter of Romans. Could it have been an autobiography of Paul? We do not know. But this is man without the Holy Spirit. The words *I, me, my, myself* are used at least thirty times in chapter seven of Romans. "We know that the law is spiritual, but I am not. I am unspiritual. I do not even acknowledge my actions as mine. For what I do is not what I want to do but what I detest. But if what I do is against my will", and so forth. I, I, I. Me, me, my. Myself. Utter confusion. Then he ends the chapter by the invocation of the Spirit. In chapter eight, which is about the Holy Spirit dwelling in us, the personal pronouns are used only about three or four times. The *I* disappears. The psychic, neurotic difficulties of our modern age are due to the effects of the Satanic and the demonic, the disruption of pattern and form. Those who are at peace are so because the Spirit is drawing all the parts of humanity together.

To illustrate the change the Spirit brings about in us, I think of a boy that I once knew. He would not comb his hair, wash behind his ears, clean his fingernails, or come to the table with clean clothes. When he went out the door, he always slammed it. One day he came down, hair combed, clean clothes, hands well-washed, and clean behind the ears. His parents could not understand it. They had begged, coaxed, pleaded, and bribed to no avail. And when he went out the door, he closed it gently. He had met Suzie. There was a new love principle introduced into his life. This is precisely what the Holy Spirit does for us. It is a love principle. Therefore it will result in a kind of spiritual impulsiveness to do good. A man who loves a woman, for example, will not give her a ring of tin instead of gold, because the gold represents a sacrifice. When we love, the Spirit inspires us, because we are possessed by love to do that which we would never do from reason. That is one of the reasons, too, why the love of the Holy Spirit is something that will prompt us to pray every day in reparation for the sins of the world.

The Spirit changes without changing   *June 8*

Sacrificial love is the gift of the Spirit, and that changes characters. If the Spirit of Christ possesses a soul, regardless of who it is, there's a new creature. An English writer named [Alfred] Noyes described a visit that he made to the home of Swinburne, the atheistic poet. Swinburne took him into the library and the poet boasted: "This is where I wrote my atheistic poetry. Glory to Man in the highest for Man is the Master of all!" Then Noyes said he began to spit out venom against the Church. Years passed, Swinburne died and went to meet his God. Years later Noyes went back to Bonchurch, where Swinburne had grown up. He saw a procession of children clothed in white, dropping flowers as they walked. He followed the procession. It went into the library of the old Swinburne home, which was now a chapel of the Sacred Heart. At the moment of Benediction, Noyes raised his eyes and noticed again the great window at the end of the library wall, with the initials of the poet's mother unchanged: I.H.S. It is thus that the Spirit changes without changing.

Test the spirit   June 9

Foster devotion to the Spirit but, as the Holy Father said, be careful that you do not confuse the psychic and the spiritual. He was referring to this passage in Hebrews: "For the word of God is alive and active. It cuts more keenly than any two-edged sword, piercing as far as the place where life and the spirit, joints and marrow divide." In other words, the Word of God makes a very keen distinction between joints and marrow (and we know how closely they are united), between the spirit and the mind, the psychical—that's the word that's used—and the spiritual. The two can be very close. We can have psychical, emotional manifestations, but as the Holy Father warned, they may only be psychical. They may not be spiritual. So test the spirit.

The Mass is a drama   June 10

What is the Mass? The Mass is a drama; it's not a tragedy because there's a Resurrection. In every great drama there is first of all the conception of it strong in the mind of the artist. Second, there are long rehearsals, the choosing of characters and types; third, there is opening night; and fourth, there are road companies. The drama of the Mass was conceived in the mind of the eternal dramatist, for the Lamb was slain from the beginning of the world. Then there were the rehearsals and the types and the choosing of characters: paschal lamb, the serpent, and the many other instances and prototypes of sacrifice in the Old Testament. Then came the opening night, the Last Supper, which looked forward to the cross. And then the Lord sent out his road companies, his priests: "Do this in memory of me." Same action, same words, same drama, only different characters pronouncing the lines. When, therefore, we begin the Mass, we are reaching back to the cross of Calvary and lifting it out of its rocks and planting it right down here in our midst. Every time a Mass is offered, Calvary is represented somewhere on earth.

Not a souvenir   June 11

The Mass is not a souvenir. When you go to Mass it is not the same as going, for example, to Calvary and chipping away a rock and saying, "This is a souvenir of the place where our Lord died." No, the Mass is a vision; it is an action in time and in eternity. It is in time, because we see it taking place before our eyes on the altar. It is also in eternity, as regards the value of redemption. All the merits of our Lord's death, Resurrection, ascension, and glorification are applied to us. We unite ourselves with that great eternal act of love. The Mass, then, is not a distinct sacrifice from the cross. If we at the Mass close our eyes and concentrate on that mystery, we are in effect with Mary, and Magdalen, and John at the foot of the cross.

The cross is here   June 12

The Mass is not a new sacrifice. It is the re-presentation in space and time of redemption. Why should we be penalized by the eternal God because of the accident of time? Are there not women today who want to be Veronicas and to offer veils to the suffering Christ? Are there not men like Simon who want to help carry the cross? Do we not want to take our own sufferings, to have them united with him in order that they might be considered part of the expiation for our sins? It is said that science might someday be able to go back and pick up all the sounds that were ever spoken because they still exist someplace in space. That means that we might recover the voice of Alexander and Gregory and Demosthenes, even the voice of Christ; but what is that compared to going back and finding and repeating the very sacrifice of the cross? What compares to taking the cross of Calvary and transplanting it to New York, London, Tokyo, and Berlin, and applying the benefits of redemption to our souls now? What a mystery of love! This is the Mass.

How God sees us   *June 13*

Lovers see one another through rose-colored glasses. At every Mass, at the time of consecration, the heavenly Father sees us through his Son. He sees us through rose-colored glasses. We are loveable; we are perfect. This is our supreme moment of relationship to the Godhead through Christ. This is our death, and this therefore is the central part of the Mass because it is Calvary. It is the condition of the Resurrection. Unless you die to yourself, you cannot live in my kingdom. We are dead, but in the Christian order death is the condition of life.

Promise of the resurrection   *June 14*

If the Mass had no communion, it would be totalitarianism, because in every communist and fascist state the person gives himself to the state and is put, as it were, in wet cement, and it hardens, and he never gets himself back. But though we die now, we are going to have a resurrection. What are we dying to? We're dying to the lower part of ourselves, the old Adam so that the Christ life, the new creature in us, will have a new risen strength. In communion, therefore, Christ is saying to us, you give me your time, I will give you my eternity. You give me your death, I will give you my life. You give me your nothingness, and I will give you my all.

Christ lives in us   *June 15*

There are two ways of knowing: knowing from the outside and knowing from the inside, knowing by study and knowing by communion. Hence, sacred scripture always speaks of the union of husband and wife as "knowledge". For example, "Adam knew Eve, and she conceived." Mary, "I know not man." Paul said, "Husbands possess your wives in knowledge." The Old Testament said, "Solomon knew her not." There is a knowledge that comes from the intimate, personal union of husband and wife that transcends any other kind of knowledge. And so in the Eucharist there is another kind of knowledge by communion that is not given to us by study. This is the incorporation to the higher life.

We live in Christ   *June 16*

Chemicals have to die to themselves to live in plants; plants have to be ground beneath the jaws of death to live in animals; and animals have to submit themselves to the knife and fire to live in man. We also have to die to ourselves to continue to live in Christ. So communion also has another aspect. Paul says, "Know you not that as often as you eat of this bread or drink of this chalice you announce the death of the Lord until he comes." This, then, is the communion where we begin now to live in Christ and become dead to the world. What a blessed privilege this is!

Mass in Dachau   *June 17*

A priest who was in the German prison camp Dachau describes the Mass after all the German guards were in bed. He said, "Our lives were in danger if we were ever discovered. A young priest had to memorize the names of all of those who had received communion, but it was forbidden for us to gather in groups for prayer. After night call and bed check, we would set our guards, darken the windows, and the lucky one to be chosen to celebrate for this momentous occasion would carefully brush his pathetic prison garb, put the stole over his shoulders, and by the small light of his smuggled candle begin the commemoration of that other great Passion of which our own was the physical continuation. We could understand the Mass. All that could crowd into the room were there, tears of joy running down our cheeks. Christ the Lord, who knew what suffering was, was coming to suffer with us, to bring us strength and consolation. The small hosts were broken into as many particles as possible so the greatest number could communicate. We had to keep a secret roster of those who received. We missed some of the liturgy perhaps, but I think that God looked down into that prison room and found a particularly refreshing response to his cry of love from the cross, 'I thirst.' There was nothing that could keep us from doing all in our power to be closer to God."

A memorial of his death   *June 18*

Our Blessed Lord's last meal is more than a meal. It is a memorial of his death. He used bread and wine because these were the two substances which traditionally nourished man.

In using bread and wine he was therefore using a symbol of ourselves. He now prepares the new passover. The old Passover was to celebrate the Jews leaving their bondage in Egypt and coming into the promised land. The new covenant, the new exodus, the new passover, is passing from sin to union with God through Christ. Our Lord then says, "I am going to give you a memorial of my death." He then symbolized for them his death by the separate consecration of his bread and wine. He said first, "This is my Body." Over the wine he said, "This is my Blood", not "this symbolizes". This *is*. That separate consecration of bread and wine was like the tearing apart of blood from body, which is the way he would die on the cross the next day. And then he said, "Do this in memory of me." Every time we assist at Mass we are watching the renewal of the death of Christ and incorporating our own death into his. That is the meaning of the Eucharist.

A sense of the holy   *June 19*

After he purified it, our Lord left the temple because the people had become irreverent. In religion it is possible for irreverence to grow. There can be a want of the sense of holy. Holy means set apart. For example, Sunday is holy. It is set apart from the rest of the week. A church is holy; it is separate and distinct from other buildings. And therefore there is a fitting conduct in the presence of God, a conduct which was lost in those days and which is lost in ours. Just think of the way that people dress coming to Mass. They would not go to the home of a visiting duke the way they come to see the Lord God of Hosts. It is easy to blame those few who trafficked in the temple, but what of the many of us who give up the signs of their dedication, for example, the nuns who would give up the sacramental signs of their dedication? Or the priests who would give up clerical dress?

Why don't the young get anything out of Mass?

Our young people are saying, "I don't want to go to Mass. I don't get anything out of Mass." Of course they don't. They don't bring anything to it. You don't get anything out of the Louvre unless you know something about art. You don't get anything out of a visit to Europe unless you know something about history. You don't get anything out of an opera unless you know something about music. What are we teaching our young people? Doctrine, doctrine, doctrine, not sacrifice or discipline? We need to tell them to bring something here. Bring a sacrifice, bring a commitment. Give up some of your time, give up some of your drink, then you'll be able to bring something more to the altar than just simply bringing up bread and wine. Begin to bring yourselves.

The Eucharist and faith in the gospel   *June 21*

The importance of the Eucharist in the gospels is manifested by the fact that there were two miracles of the multiplication of loaves and fishes: one before the Jews, the other before the Gentiles. It was as if our Blessed Lord made certain that both his own people and those who were to be his people would know this mystery.

After the multiplication of the loaves, mentioned in John 6, before the Jews our Lord said that he had come down from heaven as the bread of life and he asked, "What will you think when I ascend into heaven?" Notice the reaction among the Jews and among the disciples because of the faith that was asked of them. Think of how the heart of the Savior must have been saddened! First of all in verse 41, "At this the Jews began to murmur disapprovingly because he said, 'I am the bread which came down from heaven.'" And then as he reiterated it in verse 52, "This led to a fierce dispute among the Jews. 'How can this man give us his flesh to eat?'" In verse 61, "Many of his disciples on hearing it exclaimed, 'This is more than we can stomach! Why listen to such talk?' Jesus was aware that his disciples were murmuring about it and asked, 'Did this shock you? What if you see the son of man ascending to the place where he was before?'"

Again in verse 66, "From that time on, many of his disciples withdrew and no longer went about with him." Our Lord did not say, "Come back, we'll change everything." But rather, "*Abeant*"—Let them go. Then to the Twelve, "Will you also go away?" And then Peter spoke up saying, "Lord, to whom shall we go?" This was the reaction among the Jews. Whenever the Lord intends to give us his continued presence, there will always be some among his chosen people who will murmur, who will dispute, who will rebel, who will leave.

What do we all want? June 22

What do you want most? First, life. Honor, ambition, power, what good are these without life? At night we put out our hand instinctively in the dark ready to lose that member rather than lose that which we treasure most, our life. Then, as we continue, we find that there is something else that we want in life, and that is truth. One of the first questions we ask coming into the world is "Why?" We tore apart our toys to find out what made the wheels go round. Later on we tear apart the very wheels of the universe to find out what makes its wheels go round. We are bent on knowing causes. That is why we hate to have secrets hidden from us. We were made to know. But there's still something else we want besides life and truth. We want *love*. Every child instinctively presses himself to his mother's breast in token of affection. He goes to his mother to have his play wounds bound. Then later on, he seeks a companion like himself with whom he can share his heart. So the quest for love continues from the cradle to the grave. And yet, though we want these things, do we find them here? Do we find life here in its fullness? Certainly not.

What we were made for   *June 23*

If we are to find the source of light, we must go out to something that is pure light. If we wish to find the source of the life and the truth and the love that is in this world, we must seek out a life that is not mingled with the shadow of death; we must seek out a truth that is not mingled with the shadow of error, we must seek out a love that is not mingled with the shadow of hate, or satiety. We must seek out pure light, pure truth, pure love. That is the definition of God. In other words, that's what we want. That's what we were made for.

Sin and death   *June 24*

When does the soul die? Whenever there is the domination of the lower order over the higher order, whenever there is the domination of the individual over the community, of flesh over the spirit, of time over eternity, of the body over the soul, then there is death and that death we call sin. That is why scripture equates death in the biological order and sin in the moral order: "The wages of sin is death." If you buy an electric coffee pot, you will find instructions. The instructions may read, "Do not plug this coffee pot in when the pot is empty." Well, suppose you say, "Why should anybody tell me what to do? He's violating my constitutional rights." When you say that, you forget that the manufacturer of that coffee pot gave you instructions in order that you might get perfect coffee out of it. Sin is a deliberate violation of the law of God. When God made us he gave us certain laws, not in order to destroy our freedom, but in order that we might perfect ourselves. When we violate those laws, we break a relationship, and we hurt ourselves. That is why in the parable of the prodigal son the father said of the prodigal, "He was dead. Now he is alive."

What is atheism? June 25

Atheism is not a doctrine; it is a cry of wrath. There are two kinds of atheists. There are the simple persons who have read a smattering of science and conclude that there probably is no God. The other type of atheist is the type that might be called militant, such as the communists. They do not deny the existence of God; they challenge God. It is the very reality of God that saves them from insanity. It is the reality of God that gives them an object against which they may vent their hate.

God's knowledge of things June 26

How does God know? God does not know the way we know. We know by looking at things. God knows by looking at himself. We can get a faint idea of God's knowledge from an architect. Before an architect puts up a building, he can tell you the size of the building, its dimensions, the location of each room, its height, the number of elevators it will have, and so forth. How does he know all of this before the building is built? Because he is the designer of the building. Now God is a designer too, but God is not just a designer of the the human universe. He's *the* cause of the very being of the universe. And just as an architect need only look into his own mind to understand the nature of his building and as a poet knows his verses in his own mind, so God knows all things by looking at himself. He does not need to wait for you to turn a corner before he knows that you are doing so. He does not see little boys putting their fingers into the cookie jar and conclude they are stealing. Everything is naked and open to the eyes of God.

All time at one glance   *June 27*

We can get a faint idea of what God's knowledge is from this example. Suppose you walked through a cemetery in which you saw a succession of gravestones belonging to the same family. As you walked along slowly, you saw written on the first gravestone the inscription: Ezekiel Higgenbotham, died 1938. You walked a little further and you saw another tombstone reading: Hiram Higgenbotham, died 1903. A few steps more: Nahum Higgenbotham, died in 1883. And then still further on: Reginald Higgenbotham, died in 1861. These tombstones would indicate a succession of events that happened in space and time. Now suppose that you flew over that cemetery in a plane. Then you would see all at once. That is how history must look to one who is outside of time.

Why science works   *June 28*

Because God knows all things and because he is Creator, it follows that every single thing in the world was made according to an idea or pattern existing in the divine mind. Look round about you. You see a bridge, a statue, a painting, a building. Before any of these things began to be, they existed in the mind of the one who designed or planned them. In like manner, there is not a tree or flower, bird or insect in the world that does not in some way correspond to an idea existing in the divine mind. Their patterns have been wrapped up, as it were, in matter. What our knowledge does and what science does is to unravel and unwrap this matter in order to rediscover the ideas of God. It is because God put his ideas or patterns in things that we are assured of the rationality and purpose of the cosmos. It is that that makes science possible.

Foreknowledge and predetermination   *June 29*

In order to understand the knowledge of God, you must make a distinction between foreknowledge and predetermination. The two are not identical. God does foreknow everything, but he does not predetermine things independent of our will and our merits. Just suppose that you knew the stock market very well. Because of your superior knowledge of business conditions, you said that such and such a stock within six months would be selling ten points higher than it is now. Suppose six months later it actually sold ten points higher. Would you have predetermined and caused it to be ten points higher? Although you foreknew it, other influences were there besides your superior knowledge.

Influence   *June 30*

God knows all things, but he still leaves us with freedom. How can God influence you and still leave you free? Well, consider various kinds of influences. First, turn a key in the door. There is the impact of something material on something material and the result is the opening of a door. That is one kind of influence; the influence of a material thing on another material thing. But there is still another kind of influence. In the springtime you plant a seed in the garden. The sun, the moisture, the atmosphere, the chemicals in the earth all begin to influence that seed. It certainly is not the same kind of action as turning a piece of steel in a lock. There are tremendous capacities for growth in that seed, and what most awakens the seed to growth is something invisible, namely, the rays of the sun. Now go a stage higher. Consider the case of a father talking to his son, trying to influence him, for example, to become a doctor. What actually influences the son is some invisible truth, as well as the deep love of the father for the son and the son for the father. Love brings out in the son a free act. The son is not obliged to do exactly what his father wants; he is free to do the contrary. But truth and love have so moved him that he regards what he does as the very perfection of his personality. Later on he may say, "I owe everything I have to that conversation I had with my father. I really began to discover my true self."

July

How God works
July 1

God works upon your soul. He does not work like a key in a lock; he works less visibly than a father on a son, but his love speaks to our freedom in the same mysterious words, I and you: as one heart to another. Because God is the very embodiment of love, his love inspires you to be what you are meant to be: a free person in the highest sense of the word. The more you are led by God's love, the more you become yourself, and it is all done without ever losing your freedom.

Why God made the universe
July 2

What purpose did God have in mind in making this world? The answer is that God intended to build a moral universe. He willed from all eternity to build a stage on which *characters* would emerge. He might have made a world without morality, without virtue, without character. He might have made a world in which each of us would have sprouted goodness with the same necessity, for example, as that of the sun rising in the east and setting in the west. But he chose not to make that kind of a world, not to make a world in which we would be good, as fire is hot and ice is cold. He willed to make a moral universe so that by the right use of the gift of freedom characters might emerge. What does God care for in things tiled into an infinity of space even though they be diamonds? For if all the orbits of heaven were so many jewels, glittering as the sun, what would their external but undisturbed balance mean to him in comparison with the single character which could take hold of the tangled skein of a seemingly wrecked and ruined life and weave out of them the beautiful tapestry of saintliness and holiness?

God's choice

The choice before God in creating the world lay between creating a purely mechanical universe, peopled by mere automatons, or creating a spiritual universe in which there would be a choice of good and evil. What was the condition then of such a universe? He had to endow us with the power to say yes and no and to be captains of our own fate and destiny. Morality implies responsibility and duty, but these can exist only on the condition of freedom. Stones have no morals because they are not free. We do not condemn ice because it is melted by heat. Praise and blame can be bestowed only on those who are masters of their own will. It is only because you have the possibility of saying no, that there's so much charm in your character when you say "yes". Take the quality of freedom away from anyone, and it is no more possible for him to be virtuous than it is for the blade of grass which he treads beneath his feet to be virtuous. Take freedom away from life, and there would be no more reason to honor the fortitude of martyrs than there would be to honor the flames which kindle their stakes. Is it therefore any impeachment of God that he chose not to reign over an empire of chemicals? If God has deliberately chosen a kind of empire to be ruled by freedom rather than by force, and if we find that his subjects are able to act against his will, as stars and atoms cannot, does this not prove that he has given to those human beings the chance of breaking allegiance so that there might be meaning and purpose in that allegiance when they freely chose it? Here we have a mere suggestion about the possibility of evil.

Freedom and evil   *July 4*

A man who is free to love is free to hate. He who is free to obey is free to rebel. Virtue in its concrete order is possible only in those spheres in which it is possible to be vicious. Man can be a saint only in a world in which it is possible to be a devil. You say, "Well, if I were God, I would destroy evil." Well, if you did that, you would destroy human freedom. God will not destroy freedom. If we do not want any dictators on this earth, certainly we do not want any dictators in the kingdom of heaven. Those who would blame God for allowing man freedom to go on hindering and thwarting his work are like those who see blotches and smudges and errors in the student's notebook and would condemn the teacher for not snatching away the book and doing the copy himself. Just as the object of the teacher is sound education and not the production of neat and well-written copybooks, so the object of God is the development of souls and not the production of biological entities.

Justice as well as mercy   *July 5*

If we owe somebody twenty dollars, the debt can be forgiven, but justice is not satisfied unless we completely pay the debt. I can remember that as a boy I often used to break the window of my next-door neighbor. He would sometimes say, "Forget it." But somehow or other I never just wanted to be let off. So I would go to my piggy bank and take out my savings in order to pay for the broken window. We do not just want to be let off by God. We have a sense of our own dignity too, and we want in some way to pay the debt which we owe to God, though we are unable to pay it. However, the debt is to be paid, if justice as well as mercy are to be satisfied. That's why God had to become man.

From without, from within   *July 6*

Have you ever taken a rose petal into your fingers and pressed and squeezed it? Did you notice whether you could ever restore its tint? You could not. Lift a dewdrop from a leaf; you can never replace it. Evil in like manner is just too deep seated to be righted by a little bit of kindness and a little reason and a little tolerance. You might just as well tell a man who is suffering from consumption that all he need do is play six sets of tennis. The clock with a broken mainspring cannot repair itself. Salvation, therefore, has to come from without. Our human will is too weak to conquer its own evil. Just as the sick need medicine outside of themselves, we need a teacher for our minds, a physician for our bodies, and a redeemer for our souls. We need a redeemer from outside humanity, with all its weakness, its sin, and its rebellion. Now let's take the other side. We said that if the mainspring is broken, a new mainspring has to be supplied from without, but it must be put inside of the clock. So too, salvation must come from without humanity, but it has to be done in some way within humanity. So God had to become man in order that man would be redeemed from within.

A love without limit   *July 7*

When God with his divine nature came down to this world and took upon himself the human nature from the womb of his Blessed Mother, he took upon himself an instrument. Once God took upon himself our human nature, he could act in our name. And every one of the actions of that human nature would have an infinite value. Not a sigh, a word, a tear, a step of that human nature was inseparable from the Person of God. That is why one breath of God-made-man would have been enough to have redeemed the world. Why? Because it was the breath of God, and therefore had an infinite value. Why then did God suffer so much when he took upon himself our human nature? God's love knows no limits. The only way to prove perfect love is by surrender of all that one has in oneself. God took upon himself our human nature, and he said that he loved us unto the end, even to death.

The sickness and the cure   *July 8*

Just suppose that there were a great plague which affected a wide area of the world. Then some doctor in his laboratory found the remedy for this plague and made it available to everyone. There would be some who would seek the remedy. There would be others who would not. They might say, "How do I know he has the remedy? Why should I bother? I will cure myself." Are they not all potentially saved? It is certainly not the fault of the scientist that they are not cured. It is the fault of people themselves. So it is with the Person of Christ. He brought salvation to all men. It is up to us to find that salvation in him.

How Christ saw humanity   *July 9*

Our Lord was hopeful about humanity. He always saw men the way he originally designed them. He saw through the surface, the grime and the dirt, the real man underneath. He never identified a person with sin. He saw sin as something alien and foreign, something that did not belong to a man, something that mastered him but from which he could be freed in order to be his real self. Just as every mother sees her own image and likeness beneath the dirt on the face of her child, so God always saw the divine image and likeness beneath our sin. He looked on us much the same way a bride looks on a bridegroom the day of marriage, and as a bridegroom looks on a bride: each to the other looks the best.

The bridegroom and the bride   *July 10*

One day a woman came to me and told me that she could never love her husband again. I told her to try and think back to how much she loved him the day of their marriage, as they stood side by side at the altar. For that is the way he really was. What the woman had to do was to see, beneath the distorted image, the real person to whom she committed her life. This is precisely what our Lord does in coming to this earth. Even when men raged and stormed beneath his cross, he saw them as homeless and unhappy children of the Father in heaven. For them he grieved and for them he died. This is the vision our Lord has of humanity.

How he took our sickness   *July 11*

He took upon himself our sicknesses and our illnesses. What does sacred scripture mean by that? For about two years I pondered that passage. The answer came in reading the work of a famous Swiss psychiatrist. He tells the story of two doctors, both of whom had healing hands. One of the doctors stated that whenever he healed anyone, something of the sickness of that other person passed to himself. The other doctor stated that he often cured patients of angina, but he had to give up healing because he suffered so many attacks of angina. Is not this the key? Now let us go into some of the cures of our Lord. We often read in the gospels that when he cured the deaf, the dumb, and the blind, he sighed. We read that when he raised Lazarus from the dead, he groaned. I believe that at that moment our Lord took upon himself the ills and the sicknesses of others. When he cured a blind man, I think that he felt inside himself not just the blindness of that one man, but all the blindness of men that have ever lived.

Psychic transference   *July 12*

Jesus experienced not only physical transference, but he also suffered psychic transference. By psychic transference, I mean that he took upon himself all the loneliness of people, their mental ills, and the tragic effects of their psychoses and neuroses. He felt all of the darkness of the atheists. He knew what it was to be a skeptic and a doubter. He knew what went on in the heart of any man who raises a clenched fist, of all those who hate so much that their mouths are craters of hate and volcanoes of blasphemy. After all, if our Blessed Lord was to redeem atheists, he had to know how it felt to be an atheist, did he not? He had to feel their God-forsakenness as his own. That is why on the cross, as darkness crept into his soul, he confessed to his Father in his human nature his utter abandonment. He uttered that mysterious shriek: "My God, my God, why hast thou abandoned me?" Here he traversed the darkest valleys and deserts of mystery with all his human brothers.

Separation from God   *July 13*

When anyone says that he is forsaken by God or he denies God, he must realize that he has a brother who endured the bitterness of separation to the very last extremity of Golgotha. If he showed the way, then we can find the way out too.

This was the loneliness of Christ in the garden and the loneliness on the cross. Like a sponge, the silence of our Lord soaked up all the evil. Because he soaked it up, evil lost all of its strength. After all, when an atheist complains about the ugliness and evil of the world, does he not know in his inmost heart that this is not the way the world was intended to be? He is affirming the very existence of God by the intensity of his complaint. Without God, there would be no one to whom to complain. And in his complaint he has Christ to whom he can go.

He took on our sins   *July 14*

Some years ago a girl wrote to me telling me that at the age of eighteen she went to her first dance, in company with her cousin. After the dance, her cousin dropped her at the gate. Her house was some distance from the gate, and in the distance between the gate and the front porch, she was attacked by a stranger. In due time, she found herself with a child. The only ones who would believe her were her mother and her pastor. Neighbor women said, "Oh, isn't it terrible; the poor woman has one bad daughter." Some girls in the choir would not allow her to sing because she was wicked. She told me of all of this torture that she endured, and she said, "What's the answer?"

I wrote back to her and I said, "My dear girl, all of this suffering has come upon you because you bore the sin of one man. If you ever bore the sins of ten men, you probably would suffer ten times more. And if you ever took upon yourself the sins of a hundred men, the sufferings would be a hundred times worse. And if you ever took upon yourself the sins of all the world, you might have had a bloody sweat." That's where your sin was, and mine: in that bloody sweat

on Calvary, in this human nature that so loved us that we call
it the Sacred Heart.

A Redeemer, not a teacher   *July 15*

Our Lord was not just a teacher, but a redeemer. He was
coming to redeem man in the likeness of human flesh.
Teachers change men by their lives. Our Blessed Lord would
change men by his death. That poison of hate and sensuality
and envy which is in the hearts of men could not be healed
simply by mild exhortations of social reform. The wage of
sin is death, and therefore it is by death that sin would be
atoned for. As in ancient sacrifices where the fire symboli-
cally burned up the imputed sin along with the victim, so
on the cross the world's sin would be put away in Christ's
suffering. For he would be upright as a priest, and prostrate
as a victim. If there is anything a good teacher wants, it is a
long life which will make his teaching known. Death is always a great tragedy to a teacher. When Socrates was given
the hemlock juice, his message was cut off once and for all.
Death was a stumbling block to Buddha and stood in the
way of all of the teachings of the eastern mystics. But our
Lord was always proclaiming his death, in which he took upon
himself the sins of the world so he would appear as a sinner.

We know him in his death   *July 16*

As our Blessed Lord put it, "When you have lifted up the
Son of Man you will recognize that it is myself that you look
for." He did not even say that it was by his teaching that they
would understand. It would rather be by his personality that
they would grasp the meaning of his coming. Only then
would they know, after they had put him to death, that he
spoke the truth. His death, then, instead of being the last of

a series of failures, would be a glorious success and the climax of his mission on earth. And that's the great difference in the pictures and statues of Buddha and Christ. Buddha is always seated, eyes closed, hands folded across his fat, sleek body, intently looking inward. Christ is not seated on this earth. He's lifted up, he's enthroned. His person and his death are the heart and soul of his teaching. The cross and all that it implies is the very center of his life.

Whose inscription is on us?   *July 17*

Our Lord took upon himself a patterned human nature. That human nature was something like a die that a government makes when it wishes to mint coins. When the die is fashioned, millions of coins can be fashioned like it. Christ, our patterned man, was born; he suffered; he overcame temptations; he rose from the dead and was glorified at the right hand of the Father. Because he was born, we are to be born, not physically, but spiritually. Because he denied himself and suffered, we are to deny ourselves. The cross becomes the condition of the empty tomb. Once our life is patterned upon his crucifixion, then our life shall be patterned also on his glorious Resurrection and ascension. Are we as coins? He will ask for coins and he will say, "Whose inscription is thereon?" Is it Caesar's? Do we belong to the world? Or do we belong to God?

God's first thought   *July 18*

As we look at history as revealed in the Bible, we find that it is God who is always in search of man. It is not man in search of God. Man does seek God, but not with the same intensity with which God seeks man. Just think of how much the thought of man and the love of man is in the mind and heart of God. What is the first reflex thought we find in sacred scripture of God? Not the first description of him creating the world, but the first thought he has about himself and within himself. You might think that his first thought would be about his life and his truth and his love and yet that is not the first thought in scripture. Open Genesis, and you will find it. God's first thought about himself is, "Let us make man." Think of it: as if God could not exist without man. God does not need man to complete himself to fulfill a need, but he needs man as a kind of a gift. That is to say: he must have someone to whom he can show his love. Therefore, the first monologue that we touch in sacred scripture is the monologue of God thinking about man.

The first question   *July 19*

One of the first dialogues in scripture, the first question in scripture, is God saying to man, "Adam, where art thou?" Man, why are you hiding? Why do you run from me? The next dialogue is about the neighbor. God says to Cain, "Where is thy brother Abel?" God is immersed in the thought of man. Here we find the first two laws of God, love of God and love of neighbor, in the two questions: "Man where art thou?" and "Where is thy brother?" It was at the beginning of humanity, we find, therefore, that humanity received a call from God to communion with himself. God will not let man go.

God gets in somehow   *July 20*

In Russia there was a play called *Christ in the Morning Coat*. On the stage was a simulated altar filled with vodka bottles, with drunken priests and drunken nuns about it. An actor, whose name was Rostovich, came out to ridicule the beatitudes. He began reading, "Blessed are the poor, blessed are the merciful, for they shall receive mercy, blessed are the clean of heart for they shall see God." And he read on and on in the Gospel of Matthew. At the end he said, "I believe." It was the end of the show, and they never played it again. No one knows what has happened to Rostovich.

There are holes in the head of each and every one of us, and God's grace can get inside.

The chosen people   *July 21*

How does God deal with humanity when humanity begins to multiply? Out of all of the peoples of the world, he chooses one people who are to be his people. This group, this corporation, or this special people are to be the means of bringing salvation to everyone else in the world. Now who were his people? His people were the people of Israel, and he called them first through Abraham, and he governed them through Moses; he ruled them through the judges and the kings; he threatened, pleaded, and coaxed; he warned, and he loved through the prophets. Over and over in the Old Testament we find that God who loves humanity deals with them through this particular group. In his own words, God says in the book of Exodus, "You shall be my peculiar possession above all people. For all the earth is mine, and you shall be to me a priestly kingdom, a holy nation." And again God speaks and says, "You shall be my people, and I shall be your God."

The new people of God   *July 22*

When our Lord does come to use the word *qahal*—the word used for God's people—he calls it "my *qahal*": I will found my Church, my people. The bond that Christ establishes with this new *qahal* is not a bond of law, it is a bond of love.

The very best moment for establishing this bond was a banquet where his Twelve sat about him in love. Just as Moses often sprinkled blood upon the people as a sign of covenant, so he said that he would make a new covenant, a new pact, a new testament. And there was the sprinkling of the blood of goats and bullocks and sheep; he gave his own Blood and said, "This is the Blood of the new covenant"—the new testament, the new pact. This is the bond that will unite all of my people together. Now do you see that the Church is not an institution?

Nothing between you and God   *July 23*

Maybe you have often said, "I do not want an institution standing between God and me." Well, that's right. After all, you have a right to communicate with God. But the Church is not that kind of an institution, standing between you and God. Israel was not between the world and God. Think of the Church somewhat in the fashion of a body. Do you ever say, for example, I do not want your lips and eyes and hands and so forth standing between me and you? After all, how can I communicate anything to you, except by something visible and tangible and carnal? Anything visible that you see about me or will ever see about me is nothing but the sign of an invisible soul. The carnal is the token of the spiritual. So when our Blessed Lord came to this earth and took upon himself a human body, you would not say, "I do not want this body of Christ standing between me and my love of Christ." That is the only way of the Incarnation, to communicate the divine through the human. This human nature of our Blessed Lord, this body of his was the instrument of his divinity. When, therefore, our Lord came as priest, as prophet, and as king, everything he did was done through the power and the means of this human nature.

The best way to understand that the Church is not just an institution is to understand it as the body of Christ. That's the way St. Paul understood the Church, and that's the way we have it in sacred scripture. Our Blessed Lord says all through the gospels that he is going to establish a new body, a new *qahal*, a new people of God. After all, when people are united for a given purpose, they are a body. Now our Lord did not use the word "body" precisely because his own physical body was before everyone. He used the word "kingdom" because that was a word the Jews could understand. But when St. Paul was talking to the pagans, he had to use a word which was more understandable, namely, "body". Our Lord communicated exactly the same idea. He said that the new people he would unite with himself would be related to him as branches and vine. He said, "I am the vine, you are the branches." The truth that he had, he said he would give to them. "My truth I give to you. My power I give you." Also he communicated the power to forgive sins. Our Blessed Lord said that he would develop and form a new body which would be very small at first like a mustard seed, and then it would grow and spread throughout the entire world.

The prolongation of the Incarnation *July 25*

My own human body is made up of millions and millions of cells, and yet it is one body because it is vivified by one soul, governed by an invisible mind, and presided over by a visible head. So all who later on will be incorporated into this new body of Christ will be one because they will be vivified by one soul, the Holy Spirit, governed by an invisible mind, Christ in heaven, and presided over by a visible head, namely, the one whom Christ chose at the beginning to bear the keys of his kingdom. Therefore, this body of Christ was to be the prolongation of his Incarnation. Our Lord was to grow and expand very much like a cell. We sometimes think that a church is formed by all of us coming together and saying, "Oh, let's get together and form a church", just as we form a tennis club. That's not the way the body of Christ was formed. God's power was in the midst of his people.

How the Church grows

July 26

The body of Christ doesn't grow as a house grows, by the addition of brick to brick and door to door and wall to wall. It grows like a cell. First, there is this divine life that came to this earth, namely, God in man. It starts with the humanity of Christ, this body of his. Now he says he is going to form a new body. It will not be a moral body or a political body, so he has to give it a new name. The name that has been given to it through the centuries is "mystical" to indicate that the unity that binds it together does not come from men but from his Spirit, from himself. That was why there had to be a Pentecost: to put a soul into this body.

Formed by the Spirit

July 27

The twelve apostles that our Lord gathered to himself were very individualistic. They were very much like the hydrogen and phosphate and sulphur in a laboratory. In fact, we have in the laboratory all the chemicals that enter into the constitution of a baby. Why can we not make a baby? Because we lack that vivifying, unifying power which is a soul. So the apostles, disparate, disconnected, disjointed, could not form this body of Christ. They could be formed only by Christ and his Spirit in them. And as through the physical body of our Lord, it was God who taught, it was God who covered, it was God who sanctified.

St. Paul and the Church   *July 28*

St. Paul was a member of the old Israel, and he therefore would not accept the revelation of the new Israel, the new people of God. He started to persecute the Church. Saul decided to go to Damascus to persecute the Church there. By this time the early members of the Church were very much disturbed by this learned Saul, for that was his Jewish name. I am sure that many of the members of the Church in those days must have prayed that God would send a good coronary thrombosis to Saul. They must have said, "Dear Lord, send us someone to answer Saul." God heard their prayers. He sent someone to answer Saul. He sent Paul. That was his Roman name. On his way to Damascus, a light shone round about him. He was thrown from his beast. And he heard a voice saying, "Saul, Saul, why persecutest thou me?" Why does our Lord say *me*? He is in heaven. How can anybody persecute him? No wonder St. Paul asked, "Who art thou?" And our Lord answered, "I am Jesus, whom thou persecutest." Saul must have thought within himself, "After all I'm only persecuting the members of the Church in Damascus. How can I be persecuting you?" How? If someone steps on your foot, do not your lips complain? If someone strikes your body, does not your head protest? Christ, the Son of the living God is the head of the mystical body, the Church. Therefore, when anyone struck that body, they struck him.

A body needs a head   *July 29*

It is very strange that those who admit with scripture that the Church is the mystical body of Christ will not also admit a head. After all, how are we to know, for example, that the body exists in this earth? It is very easy to know that Christ was once walking the earth simply because men saw him. After his ascension, how would men know his mystical body and where his life was to be found? Our Blessed Lord did not leave these questions unanswered. He gave a sign that we would know his body, and the sign was the sign of all living things. How does any life manifest itself? Does not the unity of life manifest itself through the head, which is the source of the movements of the body? The head is the symbol, is it not, of the unity of life? Legs and arms can be amputated without destroying the unity of life. But cut off the head, and it is the end of life.

Not by flesh and blood   *July 30*

Concerning his confession of divinity, our Lord said to Peter, "Flesh and blood have not revealed this to thee." In other words, you do not know that I am Christ, the Son of God, by natural instincts or by reason, just as you who are reading this do not know just by reason alone that Christ is the Son of God. Your reason gives you motives of credibility, but there had to be an illumination from above. Here there's a very special illumination of Peter, because he recognizes now that Christ is not only the Messiah; he is also the Son of the eternal Father.

One church, one building   *July 31*

Next our Lord said, "I will build my Church"—my *ecclesia*, my *qahal*. He did not say, "I will build my churches." The Church is his body. Christ cannot have many bodies. That would be a physical monstrosity. The whole organic foundation of the mystical body is founded on a single man who is to have divine assistance. Notice our Lord also said, "I will *build* my church." This same word "build" is used in the book of Genesis. In the Latin translation of the scriptures, the Vulgate, exactly the same word is used to describe how Eve was formed out of Adam and how Christ built his Church. Adam was like an unfinished thing until Eve was born. So scripture says that Christ was to have his fullness in his bride, the Church. As Eve was built from Adam, so the Church was built from Christ.

August

When God said "we"

Another instance of how our Lord associated Peter with himself was in the payment of the temple tax. It is the only time in scripture where God ever associates a human being with himself under the personal pronoun *we*. Just think how proud you were when, as a child, perhaps, your father put his arms around you and said, "We will do this." Now at the time of the payment of the temple tax our Blessed Lord told Peter to pay it, and he said to pay it "for me and for thee". Then he adds, "that we may not scandalize." Here he makes himself one with Peter. Peter is associated with the Master in a way that no one else can ever be associated. We—Christ and Peter. That is why papal encyclicals begin with the word *we*.

The chain that leads to Peter

Peter's story is the story of the restored man: our model, our example. There are over two hundred fifty popes reaching back to Simon. They are links in the great pontifical chain. No chain is stronger than its weakest link, and the weakest link of the chain of popes was the first. But that weak link was held in the hands of Christ. That is why the papacy will never fall.

When our Blessed Lord gathered his apostles around him on one occasion, he said, "Satan would sift you as wheat."

This is a meaning we lose by substituting the word "you" for "thou". Our Lord said, "Satan would sift *you Twelve* as wheat. I have prayed for you"—no, that's not what the gospel says. Did our Lord say he had prayed for the Twelve? No. "I have prayed for *thee*"—for Peter—"so that after you have recovered from your fall you will strengthen your brethren." Each and every one of us wants to be in that prayer of Christ. We share in that prayer of Christ only inasmuch as we are united to Peter. The Lord prayed for him in the conflict with Satan. And in that prayer for him, the Church is strengthened. It is important in this day to trust in the prayer of Christ for Peter.

Not dogma, a Person   *August 3*

As Catholics, we do not subscribe to a system of dogmas. We begin with a Person, the Person of our Lord continued in his mystical body the Church. What is faith? Faith is the meeting of two personalities. You and the Lord. There is no adhesion to an abstract dogma, but rather a communion with a Person who can neither deceive nor be deceived. The authoritarians start with a party line. We start with our Lord, the Son of the living God, who said, "I am the truth." In other words, truth was identified with his personality. Remember when you were a child. What did you consider your home? Just a sum of commands given by either your mother or your father? It was more than that, was it not? It was the love of their personalities. Our faith, then, is first and foremost in Christ, who lives in his mystical body the Church. It is only secondarily in the explicit beliefs. If our Lord did not reveal them, we would not believe them. If we lost him, we would lose our beliefs. He comes first.

To a Catholic there is nothing credible in the Church apart from Christ who lives in it. If we did not believe that our Lord was God, if we said that he was only a good man, we would never believe in the Eucharist or the Trinity. If we believed that Jesus was simply a human being who perished in the dust, we would not believe in the forgiveness of sins. But we know that our Lord once taught, governed, and sanctified through a physical body which he took through his Mother, and now we know that he continues to teach and govern and sanctify in the mystical body which he took from the womb of humanity. His first body was overshadowed by the Holy Spirit; his mystical body was overshadowed by the Holy Spirit on Pentecost. Therefore we accept every single word of his—not just what his secretaries wrote, but we receive his living words, living through the centuries. You have heard it said, "I want no church standing between me and Christ." There is no Church standing between us and Christ. The Church is Christ, for the Church no more stands between him and us than my body stands between me and my invisible mind. The Church is what St. Augustine called the *totus Christus*—the whole Christ—and therefore his truth living through the ages. Thank God for your faith, your faith in the Person of Christ who is the eternal contemporary.

Love, not fear *August 5*

It is true that in every single system of authoritarianism fear is the basis of obedience. But because we start with the Person of Christ, the basis of our obedience is not fear, it is love. You cannot love dialectical materialism, but you can love a person. Between our Lord and us there is the bond of love.

These two are inseparable. That is why our Lord did not communicate to Peter the power of ruling and governing his Church until Peter told our Lord three times that he loved him. The power to command in the Church comes only from obedience to Christ. Therefore, the submission that we as Catholics make to the Church is something like the submission that we make to one of our most devoted friends. It is like the obedience of a son to a loving father. We do not feel any distance between our Lord and us. As a pupil becomes more and more attached to his teacher by absorbing more of the truths of the teacher, so too, the more we become more and more united to Christ, the more we love him and also the more truth we absorb. The more we know our Lord, the more we obey the truth manifested through his Church, and the less we fear. That is why scripture says, "Perfect love casts out fear." The more his truth abounds, the more we love him.

Who are "they"? *August 6*

I really cannot imagine anything more cold and more enslaved, more paralyzing to human reason or destructive of freedom than that thing to which millions of people are prostrating themselves every day, namely, the terrible, anonymous authority of "they". "They say". "They are wearing green this year." "They say that Catholics adore Mary." "They say that the hair will be worn shorter this year." "They say that Freud is the thing." Who are *they*? Countless slaves and puppets are bowing down daily before that invisible, tyrannical myth of *they*. No wonder dictatorships arose to personalize that terrible slavery. These millions will not accept the authority of Christ who rose from the dead, who continues to live in the Church. We know whom we obey. Millions do not know whom they are obeying. They cannot point to the persons or the object behind that terrible, anonymous "they". But thank God we know. We obey our Lord in the Church.

When love fails   *August 7*

A very negative proof that love is what binds us is found in the thousands and thousands of letters that I have received in the course of the years from persons who have fallen away from the Church or are outside of her because they entered into a second or third invalid marriage. All of these letters invariably express a great unhappiness on the inside: a boredom, an *ennui*, a disgust, and an anxiety, not because the letter writers have broken a law, but because they have broken a bond of friendship with Christ. Their loneliness also bears witness to the truth that when there is no person to love, there is no certitude. There's only subjection. When there is the love of Christ, then love begins to believe everything. And since no one can ever surpass the love that Christ showed for us in redeeming us and founding his mystical body the Church, there can be no greater certitude in the world. That is the only kind of love that can save us from authoritarianism with its fear, and make us really loving creatures bound together by the tendrils of affection to him who loved us even to the point of death.

Does truth destroy freedom?   *August 8*

Is it true that the more you subscribe to divine truth, the less free you become? Before I went to school I was free to believe, for example, that Shakespeare was born in 1224. But finally, I was told that Shakespeare was not born in 1224, but rather in 1564. I found out that education in truth was really restricting my freedom to fall into error. Before I went to school I also thought that "H_2O" was really the initials of a spy. Then I fell into the hands of a reactionary teacher. He stopped all of my liberalism. Do you know what he told me H_2O meant? He said it was the symbol for water. Thus, the more I studied, the freer I became to know error.

The truth shall make you free   *August 9*

The only reason for being free from something is to be free *for* something. Freedom, therefore, is not liberation from the truth, it is, rather, the acceptance of the truth. When are you really most free? When you know the truth about something. For example, you are free to draw a triangle on the condition that you give it three sides and not thirty-three. You are free to draw a giraffe if you draw it with a long neck. If you do not accept the truth about the nature of giraffes and, instead, give your giraffe a short neck, you will find that you are not free to draw a giraffe. You are free to drive your automobile in traffic on the condition that you obey the traffic laws. You are free to pilot a plane on the condition that you respect the laws of gravitation and you acknowledge the truth of aviation. That is what Jesus meant when he said, "The truth will make you free."

We have the map   *August 10*

Now our truth, therefore, in the Church is a truth that is come down to us from Christ. It is a truth that is so noble that when we begin to wander away from it, we lose our way. There's a tremendous satisfaction in having a map. That is what the truth of Christ is like in the Church. We may get off the road; we may get off it by sin, we may get off it by error. But as long as we have that map, we can get back on the road. There are indeed some people who once they get off the road, tear up the map. That is a still greater tragedy.

Both sides of the question   *August 11*

The Church is very wise because she always teaches us both sides of a question. I taught philosophy in a university for twenty-five years, and I noticed that everyone who taught in the university always knew both sides of a question. For example, everyone in the Catholic university where I taught knew the opinions of the modern world. In philosophy, for example, we knew Marx and Sartre and Heidegger and Jaspers and Freud and the like. But do you think that the teachers in secular universities knew anything about Christian thought? They only know one side of the question, not both. Look at the papal encyclical on communism. A communist once told me that the clearest and finest explanation of communism he ever read was contained in the Holy Father's encyclical on communism. He gave both sides of the question. Look at that great work of philosophy and theology called the *Summa Theologica* of St. Thomas. Every single question that great mind teaches begins with a doubt and a difficulty. Then he answers it. We know both sides of the questions. Those outside of the Church know only one side. And frequently it's the wrong side.

Dependence in love   *August 12*

Our freedom, therefore, is not an independence of truth, but rather dependence in love. That is the joy of being a Catholic. Perhaps I can make it clear with this analogy. On an island in the sea there were children. Around the island were great high walls. Inside those walls the island children sang and danced and played. One day some men came in a rowboat to that island. They were reformers, and they said to the children, "Who put up those walls? Someone is restraining your freedom. Tear them down." The children tore them down. Now if you go back, you will find all of the children huddled together in the center of the island, afraid to play, afraid to sing, afraid to dance, afraid of falling into the sea. That is the Church, the wall is truth, and as Christ said, "If the Son of Man makes you free, you are free indeed."

What is wrong   *August 13*

If we are to find a total explanation of what is wrong with man, it must be sought within man himself. When we see a monkey acting crazily in a zoo, we do not say, "Oh, do not act like a nut." But when we see a man acting foolishly we say, "Don't act like a monkey." You see, a monkey cannot stoop lower than itself, but man can. Because man is spirit as well as matter, he can descend to the level of beasts, though never so completely as to destroy the image of God that is in his soul. It is this possibility that allows the peculiar tragedy of man. Man would never be frustrated, he would never have an anxiety complex, if he were an animal and if he were made just for this world. Because of that summit, that peak, that desire for perfect happiness which he does not attain, he can become the seat of conflict.

Why the commandments?   *August 14*

It is true that God has established the law. There will be a moral universe. A moral universe implies a free universe; because we are free, we can abuse our freedom. But we are not to blame God for it. When you buy an automobile, you always find with it a set of instructions. The manufacturer tells you the pressure to which you ought to inflate your tires and the kind of oil you ought to put in your crankcase and the kind of gasoline you ought to put in the gas tank. He doesn't give you these directions because he holds a grudge against you. And God doesn't give us commandments because he holds a grudge against us. The manufacturer of the automobile really wants to be helpful when he gives us these laws. He wants you to get the maximum utility out of that car. And God is anxious that we get the maximum amount of happiness out of life. So he said: I will tell you what you should do, what you ought to do. We are free; we can do just as we please. We ought to put gasoline into the tank of our car. But we can put perfume in there, we can put in Chanel No. 5, and there is no doubt that it is going to be nicer for our nostrils if we fill the tank with perfume rather than gasoline. But the car simply will not run on Chanel No. 5. In like manner, we were made to run on the fuel of God's love and commandments, and we simply will not run on anything else. We just bog down.

God is not a dictator   *August 15*

God refuses to be a totalitarian dictator. Therefore, he refuses to abolish evil by destroying human freedom. Instead of conscripting man, God willed to consult humanity as to whether or not it wanted to be made a member of the divine orchestra once more. An angel comes to a woman whose name is Mary and asks her in the name of God, "Will you give to God a man? Will you give to God a new note of humanity with which he can write a new symphony?" This new man must be a man, otherwise God would not be asking in the name of humanity. But he also must be outside the current of infection to which all men are subject. Being born of a woman, he would be a man, and being born of a virgin, he would be a sinless man. So the virgin was asked if she would consent to be a mother. And she gave to God a man. Her answer was, "Be it done to me according to thy word." Nine months later the Eternal established its beachhead in Bethlehem. He who was eternal appeared in time, and his name is Jesus Christ, God and Man. He is God; therefore, whatever he does has an infinite value. And though this human nature of his is sinless, he makes himself responsible for all the sins of the world.

What is grace? August 16

There is something else in the world besides poor, weak human nature. There is grace. Grace is this higher wisdom, a higher power that can come to us. The word grace, or *"gratis"*, merely means that it is free. We cannot merit it in the strict sense. It appears repeatedly in the New Testament. In the Greek, its name is *charis*. And it is mentioned about one hundred fifty times. If there is another life above the purely natural or human, then it is possible for every Christian to lead a double life, a real double life: a natural life and a divine life; a human life, and a spiritual life.

How to change direction August 17

If we are to change our direction, a new power is needed. For example, if I take a ball and throw it across the room, the ball will continue in a straight line unless some superior power averts it. So too, natural human beings continue in certain directions, as Paul would have continued his persecution. Sinners would continue in their sin. Agnostics would continue in their doubt unless some superior power intervened. And that is the power of grace.

The body is a temple   *August 18*

What does grace do to our human nature? First of all, it makes the body a temple of God. That is one of the reasons for purity. What is a temple? A temple is a place where God dwells. Remember when Jesus went into the temple of Jerusalem and the Pharisees asked for a sign, and our Blessed Lord said, "Destroy this temple and in three days I will rebuild it." He was not speaking of that earthly temple, he was speaking of the temple of his body, because in that human nature of Christ, God dwelt. By our participation in that divine life he dwells in us. That's why the body is sacred. That's why we have reverence for it. The body is not a worm, something vile. It is his temple, and one day it will be glorified too.

The light of faith   *August 19*

When grace comes into the intellect, it comes as a kind of a light. It is difficult to describe what it does to the human mind. Picture sunlight shining through a stained-glass window. Notice how it is diffused and brings out all of the color. That is what grace does to the intellect. It gives it a new vision. Faith, then, becomes to reason something like a telescope is to the eye. It does not destroy the eye, it just perfects it. When faith gets into us, it gives us a new certitude beyond reason. My arguments do not give you certitude. That has to come from faith, that has to come from God. That is why our Blessed Lord said to Peter, "Flesh and blood have not revealed this to thee, but my Father who is in heaven." The certitude that comes from faith is so great that nothing can destroy it. As a matter of fact, the certitude that comes from faith is greater than the reasons for faith. That is because the light comes from God. We often have many certitudes that are stronger than the reasons we can give. For example, if we were challenged all of a sudden to prove that we were legitimate children, it might be rather difficult. We do not have the documents. But nothing could shake our certitude. Even so, a learned man could give many arguments against the existence of God and the divinity of Christ to one of our children, but he could never destroy the faith of that child.

A new outlook on life · August 20

Not only does faith give certitude, but it also gives us a new outlook, a new outlook on birth, suffering, death, joy, pleasure, literature, and art. Those who have what St. Paul calls the carnal mind cannot understand the things of faith. It is very much like trying to make a blind man understand color. Very often, those who lack the gift of faith wonder why it is that we are so certain about life. Why do we have this outlook on suffering? Why are we not depressed? Why do we not contemplate suicide? Well, it is simply because we see things more clearly. We have a light that they don't have. A man has the same eyes at night that he has in the day. But he does not see at night. Why? Because he lacks the light of the sun. Let two people look at the same problem. They see it very differently. It is because one has only his reason and his senses, and the other has faith.

Grace and the will · August 21

When grace comes into the will, it gives us new power, new strength that we never had before. It gives us a new ability to resist temptation. Too often in this world as soon as anyone becomes a slave of sin, we speak of him as having a compulsion. We say, "Oh, he is a compulsive drinker." "He is a compulsive eater." Now that is true. The word that our Lord used to explain that compulsion was slavery. But this does not mean that these people have completely destroyed their freedom. Believe me, there is always a little area of freedom left in an alcoholic or in anyone who is given over to the slavery of sin. Sins which started with free acts of our own weaken our will, but they do not completely destroy it. It is possible for grace to establish a beachhead. Grace has its D-Day, and God can get in to anyone. After all, when we are trying to cure people of vices, we can never drive out a vice. We can only crowd it out. How do you crowd it out? You crowd it out by putting in something else. The grace of God comes in. When we begin to love him, then these vices begin to be pushed out. Once a new love comes in, we are changed.

Goodness   *August 22*

What makes a thing good? A thing is good when it attains the purpose for which it was made. I have before me now a watch. Is it a good watch? How will I know whether it is good? By asking what the purpose of a watch is. The purpose of a watch is to keep time. Does it keep time? Yes. Therefore, it is a good watch. Now let us apply that to our ultimate end. Why were we made? What is the purpose of living? The purpose of living is to be supremely happy. How do we become supremely happy? By attaining the life and truth and love which is God.

What is right?   *August 23*

There is an organ in my home. As I look at the notes on that organ, I could ask, which note is good and which note is bad? Which note is right and which note is wrong? One cannot say that any particular note is right or any particular note is wrong. What makes any note right or wrong? Its correspondence to a standard. Once I have a piece of music before me, I know what I ought to do, what note I should hit, what note I ought not to hit. So too, we have a moral standard within us which is our conscience. What is good and bad is in relationship to that standard which is not of our own making. We do not draw our own maps, and decide what the distance from Chicago to New York will be, for instance. We do not arbitrarily set our own watches. We set them by a standard outside of us. When we buy material, for example, we do not decide that a yard will be twenty-four inches instead of thirty-six inches. A good, therefore, is that which helps us in relationship to the attainment of purposes and goals and destinies which are in accordance with right reason.

Badness   *August 24*

What makes a thing bad? Well, here is a pencil. This is a good pencil; it writes. That was why it was made. Is it a good can opener? It certainly is not. Suppose I use it as a can opener. What happens? First of all, I do not open the can. I do not attain the purpose for which I used the pencil. Second, I destroy the pencil. Now if I, for example, decide to do certain things which I ought not to do, I do not attain the purpose for which I was created. For example, becoming an alcoholic does not make me happy. Furthermore, I destroy myself, just as I destroyed the pencil in using it to open a can. When I disobey God, I do not make myself very happy on the inside, and I certainly destroy any peace of soul that I ought to have.

Evil is a parasite   *August 25*

Evil is not positive. Evil is either an excess or a defect of
what is good. Food is good. Too little of it is bad; too much
of it is bad. Drink is good. Too little of it is bad; too much
of it is bad. Sleep is good. However, when sleep interferes
with duty, it is not good. Evil is very much like darkness. It
is the absence of light. It has no purpose outside itself. Rather,
it has no substance of its own. That is a better way to put it.
All badness is spoiled goodness. A bad apple is a good apple
that became rotten. Because evil has no capital of its own, it
is a parasite that feeds on goodness. Living in this universe,
with reason and will, we can see that this universe is a veil of
soul-making. We were made to be good; we were made to
attain the truth.

The limitations of the greatest minds   *August 26*

Look at the limitations of our reason: how poor it is! Even
those with very good powers of reason have admitted in the
end that they have captured just a little of truth. The great
scientist Isaac Newton said that he felt as if he were standing
on the seashore of infinite truth and the vast waters of knowledge stretched endlessly before him. Socrates, one of the
wisest of the Greeks, said, "There is only one thing that I
know and that is that I know nothing." Thomas Aquinas,
who was the greatest mind that ever lived, said at the end of
his life that all he had written seemed to him as so much
straw in comparison to a dim vision that he received of heaven.

The confusion of today   *August 27*

Look at the weak reason of people today—their confusion
of mind, their failure to even recognize any such thing as

truth or goodness. They will read one book on Monday and will say, "Oh, I'm a materialist." Then they'll read another book on Tuesday and become communists. They'll read another book later on in the week and reject both of these systems. They are laying down tracks one day and tearing them up the next. They are planting seeds one week and tearing the seeds up the next. They never work toward one goal. No wonder there are so many psychotics and neurotics in our world. They are just rehashing a lot of old errors and giving them new labels, calling some of the old errors very novel, just because they do not know they are ancient.

The laws of nature   *August 28*

Miracles are not a violation of the laws of nature. God and the universe are not on opposite sides. For example, nearly all the great railroad stations with junctions of tracks and lines running side by side have in their midst a control tower. From that little building all lines are directed and signals sent in various ways. Pull a lever and the mighty train passes on its appointed way. The working of another lever sends a freight train into a siding until the express train has passed. All railway traffic would be disorganized if the important work were not carried on in that control tower. In fact, there would be disorder and collisions. This is a feeble illustration of the laws of nature. The whole universe works upon fixed lines. We cannot see God's signals nor understand how he conveys his power to the forces of nature. We do not see him work his levers. We only know that his laws obey him with an exactness and a promptness unknown in any railway system of the world.

Miracles reveal who Christ is   *August 29*

Christ worked miracles as signs to convince men that he was
the one that was promised. He never worked a miracle to
amaze a multitude. He never worked a miracle to satisfy his
hunger or his thirst. He never worked a miracle to obtain a
living. He never received money for the things which he
accomplished. He refused to convert the stones of the
wilderness into bread to satisfy his own hunger or to cause
water to gush out of a rock to slake his thirst. Instead, he
asked a woman to let down her bucket to give him a drink.
Our Lord explained why he worked miracles. He said, "If
I act like the Son of my Father, then let my actions convince
you where I cannot. So you will recognize and learn to believe that the Father is in me and I in him."

Christ's miracles never denied   *August 30*

There is nothing silly or unreasonable in any of the miracles
of our Blessed Lord. They were subject to the tests of everyone. The vast majority of the miracles took place not in the
secret places of people's lives, but in what might be called
the physical world where they could be verified scientifi-
cally. Our Lord never performed a miracle unless there were
witnesses present. When he healed the leper, there was a
great multitude following him. In the healing of the centurion's servant, he did not even go where the servant was
dying. When he raised Peter's mother-in-law from her sick-
bed, the apostles and other people were present. Our Lord
never went up into a mountain to perform some miracle
alone. His works were accomplished before the eyes of mul-
titudes of people. That is why none of the miracles of our
Lord were ever actually denied, not even his Resurrection.

The apostles were forbidden by the authorities to teach it and preach it, but the miracle itself was never denied.

Signs of the Kingdom   *August 31*

The miracles of our Lord are inseparable from his Person. His miracles differed from that of prophets and others inasmuch as theirs were answers to prayers, granted by a higher power. But his flowed from the majestic life that was vested in him. That is why St. John calls them, in his gospel, "signs" or "works", meaning that they were the sort of thing that might be expected from the Son of God. They were evidences of Jesus' divine revelation. But they were even more, for they testified to his redemptive action as the Savior of the world. By healing the palsied and the lame and the blind, Christ clothed with visible form his power to cure spiritual diseases. These physical diseases were to him symbols of that which was spiritual. He often passed from the physical fact of the miracle to its symbolic and spiritual meaning. For example, blindness was a symbol of blindness to the light of faith. By casting out devils from those who were possessed, he pointed out his victory over the powers of evil, whereby men would be freed from slavery to evil and restored to moral liberty.

September

Is Christ a deceiver? September 1

If you expel miracles from the life of Christ, you destroy the identity of Christ and the gospels. Even a neutral attitude toward the miraculous element in the gospels is impossible. The claim to work miracles is not the least important element of our Lord's teachings. Nor are the miracles wrought by him merely an ornament to his life. They are interwoven with his entire life. The moral integrity of our Lord's character is dependent upon the reality of his miracles, because if he were a deceiver, he would not be what he claimed to be. Therefore, we cannot put asunder two things which God has joined together, namely, the beauty of Christ's character and the reality of the miracles that he worked.

A higher power than nature September 2

When a miracle seems to be at variance with a law like the universal law of gravitation, a higher power has been introduced. The law of gravitation can actually be overcome by the right arm of a little child. According to the natural laws, the ball ought to fall to the ground when it is bounced, but the hand of the little child can stop the operation of the law of gravitation by catching the ball. When God, therefore, puts forth the strength of his arm, he can suspend the action of some of the laws that he has made in order to manifest some of his goodness and his justice and the fact that he is Lord of creation.

How does grace come? *September 3*

We receive millions of graces, called actual graces. Everyone receives them, not only Christians. Every Muslim, every Buddhist, every communist in the world receives actual grace. But to be united with God we need what is called habitual grace, a more permanent grace, that which creates in us a likeness that remains. How is this grace communicated to us? How does it get into the soul? Perhaps you have seen signs on roadways. They are often painted on rocks and read, "Jesus saves." Yes, indeed he does. But the very practical question is how? We have a span of more than twenty centuries between the life of our Lord and our days. Yes, he is God. But how does he pour and infuse his divine life and power into our souls? He does it by means of the sacraments.

The sacramental principle *September 4*

We can define the word "sacrament" in a very broad way. In Greek it means "mystery". But a sacrament is any material or visible thing that is used as a sign or a channel of spiritual communication. We will go back about as far as we can to explain mysteries. We might say that the Lord made this world with a sense of humor. What do we mean by "a sense of humor"? We mean he made it sacramentally. We say a person has a sense of humor if he can see through things. We say a person has no sense of humor if he cannot see through things. We say he's too thick. Now God made this world with a sense of humor, in the sense that we were always to see him through things, as the poets do. We would look out on a mountain and think of the power of God; on the sunset, and think of the beauty of God; on a snowflake, and dwell on the purity of God. Notice that we would not be taking this world as seriously as do the materialists, to whom a mountain is just a mountain, a sunset is just a sunset, and the snowflake is just a snowflake. The serious-minded people of this world write only in prose. But those who have this penetrating glance of perceiving the eternal through time, the divine through the human, have what we call a sacramental outlook on the universe.

Natural sacraments

There are certain signs and events in our daily life which are a kind of natural sacrament. Take, for example, a word. A word has something audible about it and at the same time something unseen, invisible. If, for example, I tell a joke and if it were a very amusing one, you might laugh. But if I told it to a horse, a horse would not even give a horselaugh. Why? Because you get the meaning. That's because you have a soul, reason, and an intellect. A horse lacks that spiritual perceptive power and hence does not get the meaning. So it is with a handshake. A handshake is something visible, material, fleshy, but there is also something spiritual about it, namely, the communication of greeting and welcome. If I take my right hand and lay it upon my left, this is not a handshake. It has the visible aspect about it, most certainly, namely, the clasping of hands, but it lacks that invisible element which is the communication of personal warmth. A kiss is a kind of sacrament. It is something visible, and at the same time something invisible, namely, the communication of love.

Sacrament and architecture

Have you noticed how devoid of decoration our modern architecture is? What a contrast to the cathedrals where there were all material things, even cows and angels, sometimes little devils peering around corners! The ancient architecture was always using material things as signs of something spiritual. But today our architecture is flat, nothing but steel and glass, almost like a crackerbox. Why? Well, because our architects have no spiritual message to convey. The material is just the material, nothing else, hence no decor, no significance, no meaning, no soul. I wonder if decor and decoration in architecture has not passed out of the world at the same time politeness has. We certainly are not as polite in this century as we were in other centuries. Possibly the reason is because we no longer believe that persons have souls. They are just other animals, and hence, they ought to be treated as means to our ends. When you believe that in addition to a body there is a soul, then you begin to have great respect and reverence for personality.

Christ was the great sacrament

Christ himself was the great sacrament because he was the Word made flesh. He was the God-man. We would have seen a man, but we would have known that he was the Son of God. Therefore, Christ is the supreme sacrament of history. His human nature was the sign of his divinity. We saw God through his body. We see eternity through his time, and a loving God in the form of a man who was like us in all things, save sin. Our Blessed Lord took his human nature to heaven. Once he was glorified in heaven, he became our mediator, our intercessor, our high priest who can have compassion for us and on us because he passed through our temptations and our sufferings and our trials. Because he is God as well as man, he is going to pour down upon us from heaven his truth, his power, his grace, his life. How will he do it? He will not do it through what we might call his "bodiness", because that is already glorified in heaven. He will do it through things and also through human natures. He will use certain things in this world as extensions of his glorified body. These things might be water, bread, and oil, and so forth—channels or vehicles for the communication of his divine life.

Christ works in the sacraments   *September 8*

The reception of the grace that is in the sacraments is very effective in our soul because it is Christ who confers the grace. By the mere fact, for example, that we turn on the faucet, water comes out. The water does not come because we subjectively believe that water will come forth. The divine life of Christ is poured into our soul by the mere fact that we receive the sacrament. Of course, we must not put an obstacle in the way of receiving the sacraments. But it is *Christ* who baptizes; it is *Christ* who forgives sins. There are ministers, of course, and there are bishops and priests, but we loan Christ our eyes and our hands and our limbs. It is he who gives the grace. That, incidentally, is why, even though you received the sacrament from an unworthy priest, it would still be a sacrament. Sanctification does not depend upon the priest. Because sunlight comes through a dirty window, sunlight is not polluted. A messenger may be very ragged, but he can still bear the message of a king.

The riches of the laity   *September 9*

The greatest untapped reservoir of spiritual power is to be found in the Christian laity. It is mainly through the laity that the Church enters into the world. Lay men and women are the meeting place of the Christian and the non-Christian. They are the bond between the sacred and the profane, the religious and the secular. The laity fulfill their Christian vocation in the world. When they come to church, they receive life and truth and grace, but they receive these things for service: service in the world. In the world, this Christian truth and grace and life encounters other men and women who may lack it or certainly its richness. A Christian vocation is the exercise of the ordinary manifestation of life in such a way that the glory of God is made manifest.

Dangers for the laity   *September 10*

There is a two-fold danger. On the one hand, the Christian laity may form a kind of a ghetto; that is to say, they may consider their religious activities to be confined only to the Church and keeping the commandments. Then Christians huddle together in a kind of igloo, completely divorcing faith and action. The other extreme would be to become so worldly, that they can do nothing with it. The result of this separation of religion and the world is that culture has emancipated itself from Christ and become demonic. For the laity to be effective, they have to do three things. First of all they have to be conscious of the fact that they are members of the people of God, the community. Second, they must be theologically literate. St. Peter said they should be able to give reason for the faith that is in them. And then third, they must communicate with the world as Christians.

Not just church on Sunday   *September 11*

No one can expect to fulfill the Christian vocation with any kind of personal integrity in the modern world unless he is at home with computers, with slums, with race problems, with world affairs, with everything. The laity stand at that point where the gospel intersects the world, just as the cross stood at the intersection of the cultures of Athens, Jerusalem, and Rome. The laity cross all frontiers. They do this in the name of Christ. As we see the laity coming into church on Sundays, we ask them, do you really love one another? Are you a unified element in the community? Are you coming together just to fulfill an obligation, trying to avoid mortal sin rather than to come in to strengthen and feed a life which you ought to spread? Are you seeking a kind of selfish sanctification, forgetful that our Blessed Lord said, "For their sakes do I sanctify myself." Will you be just like everyone around you, except for this weekly habit of coming to church? When others look at this band of the faithful, will they think "I ought to be like them; I ought to have their love and their truth, and their inner peace"? Too often it is just the opposite.

Make Christ known to the world   *September 12*

The laity will have to comprehend that our Blessed Lord was not crucified in the cathedral, between two candles, but in the world, on a roadway, in a town garbage heap at the crossroads. There were three languages written on the cross; they were Latin and Hebrew and Greek, but they could have just as well been English, or Bantu, or Afrikaans. It would make no difference. Jesus placed himself at the very center of the world, in the midst of smut and thieves and soldiers and gamblers, and he was there to extend pardon to them. This is the vocation of the laity: to make Christ known in the world.

Take Christ to your neighbors   *September 13*

There are empty vessels all around us. They can be filled with the love of Christ. Are there any empty vessels in your home? Among your neighbors? If you are a lawyer, do you know empty vessels in your profession? There's a doctor; there's a nurse; are there not many whose lives are destitute? I recently heard of a lawyer who died in Berlin. He was a nonbeliever. He had a Catholic law partner, and when his friend became ill the Catholic lawyer visited him and said, "Now that you are about to die, do you not think it's time to make your peace with God?" The dying partner said to him, "If Christ and your Church has meant so little to you during your life that you never once spoke to me about it, how can it mean anything to me at my death?"

Our lack of feeling   *September 14*

Something that has particularly characterized our age is what might be called "de-eucharistization", a decline in the love of the Eucharist. It started when some theologians, completely misunderstanding the Vatican Council, felt that there was no such thing as the presence of Christ in the Sacrament and even cast some doubt on the value of it. So we suffer from what the whole world is suffering. St. Paul calls it a want of feeling. Sociologists tell us that family life and relationships between people have very much degenerated. There is a want of sensitivity and delicacy toward one another. Maybe the grossness of our carnal age has made us put less stress upon those common courtesies and urbanities which make up life. Little affection is shown between husband and wife, between mother and children, or between father and children. I mean a show of affection; there is love in providing for them, but the manifestation of love has gone into decline.

And it leads to a decline in the spiritual order. We have become poor lovers of God. We are not sensitive and responsive.

Coming to the sacrament   *September 15*

The Lord has his Sacrament. It's very much like marriage. The marriage act of husband and wife is a kind of sacrifice because the lover dies to himself and submits to the beloved. The beloved dies to herself and submits to the lover, and out of that mutual death there comes the ecstasy of love. That is the sacrifice. Do a husband and wife have a love that is only manifested in that sacrificial act? Are there not any courtesies of companionship which would even surpass in the quiet silence the ecstasy of two in one flesh? As Maeterlinck said: A friend is one in whose presence you can keep silence. As a matter of fact, their happiness, one with another, depends upon the deep consciousness that each one is a sacrament of the other. So our Lord has a Sacrament. He is really and truly present, Body and Blood, soul and divinity in the holy Eucharist. And if we know how to love, we become sensitive and responsive, and when we come into visit him, he will talk to us. We take on his likeness; as Moses' face shone because he was with God. So, too, St. Paul tells us that we grow in splendor because we are in the presence of God. Moses' splendor grew as he returned again to the mountain; this splendor rises in us, because we return to Christ. We reflect, says St. Paul, as in a mirror, the splendor of the Lord, and thus we are transfigured into his likeness, from splendor to splendor. That is what the Eucharist does.

The cross, sign of contradiction   *September 16*

The cross itself, just that figure, is the symbol of absurdity, because the upright bar of life is contradicted by the horizontal bar of death. The ego is contradicted by the other-ego, the negation of identity. By itself, it is the symbol of absurdity. But if you put someone on it, who teaches the lesson that death is the condition of life, then the cross is no longer absurd. Then it becomes a philosophy of life.

We stand beneath the cross

September 17

Besides apathy and antipathy, there was empathy, the few chosen souls at the foot of the cross. You see, the cross unites not only the friends of our Lord, the cross unites enemies. We will begin to see as the world goes on, a new kind of bigotry. We will be opposed not because we believe, for example, in the supremacy of the Holy Father, but because we are standing in the way of the demoralization of the world. We stand for life against death. We stand for the family against divorce. We stand for purity against fornication. We stand for goodness instead of vice. We are the great obstacle to the world. The new bigotry will see that cross and will hate us. So we have to be prepared for it, and we have to take our stand underneath it.

Two classes of people

September 18

I believe that there are only two classes of people in the world: those who are on the cross with Christ, and those who are beneath it to harangue him. Those who are on the cross, even by sympathy, like his Blessed Mother, are those who suffer. Take, for example, the hungry, a large percentage of the population of the world. They are on the cross. They may not know it, but that is the way they will be saved. Then there are the others who are beneath it saying, "Come down and we will believe."

Judgment is recognition

What is judgment? Judgment is recognition: recognition from our point of view and recognition from God's point of view. It is recognition, first of all, from our point of view. Suppose that we are cleaning our house when a distinguished visitor is announced. We will say, "Oh, I am not clean, wait until I wash up and dress." That's the way we are when we go before the sight of God: let me clean up a bit. Recognition is also from God's point of view. Grace is the similarity of our nature to God's nature. St. Peter says, "We are partakers of God's nature." Just as our parents know us because we share their nature, so God looks upon us. If he sees his nature in us, then he will say, "Come, come ye blessed of my Father. I am the natural Son; you are the adopted son. Come into the kingdom prepared for you." If, however, he looks and does not see that likeness of nature, as a mother knows the neighbor's child is not her own, so the Lord will say, "I know you not." It is a terrible thing not to be known by God.

We offer ourselves in the Mass

In the offertory, the people participate very often by bringing up bread and wine. The bread and wine represent the priest and the people. There has to be some symbol by which we all can stand at the altar, because we are offering ourselves to God. We're not attending a prayer. This is a sacrifice. So the good Lord has chosen something that does symbolize very well our life. Namely, bread gives us substance and wine is the very marrow of the earth, it gives us blood. When, therefore, we bring that which gives us our nourishment, we are equivalently bringing ourselves. We are on the altar. But we are not just there as offerers. The wheat had to be ground. The grapes had to be crushed. This is already an intimation of what is going to happen during the Eucharist.

The eternal sacrifice   *September 21*

This death of Christ is an eternal act. We temporalize it; we spatialize it. Think of a great log that has been sawed in two. We see a number of circles on either side of that cut log. Those circles, we know, run all the way up through the log. That's the sacrifice of Christ. It runs through history, from the very beginning, when God made an animal skin for the first parents to hide their shame; it runs through all of the symbolic sacrifices of the Jews; and it runs up to Calvary and from Calvary on into heaven itself. In fact, it began with the Lamb: slain, as it were, from the beginning of the world. Now we redo that sacrifice. Scripture says that Christ can never die again. If Christ can only die once, why do we say the Mass is a sacrifice and he dies again? Of course our Lord can never die again in the human nature which he took from Mary. But at the beginning of every Mass, he looks out and says: Peter, Paul, Mary, John, Ann, give me your human natures. I will die again in you, and your death will be the pledge of your resurrection, as mine was the model.

Christ interceding in the Mass   *September 22*

The Eucharist demands the Resurrection; the Body and Blood of Christ is the risen Christ mediated through his Holy Spirit. Here I am only using a kind of a scenic example, but it may help us in the simplicity of our faith. When the Holy Sacrifice of the Mass is offered, one can imagine the divine Son in heaven saying to his Father while showing his scars, "See how much I love them. Have mercy on them. Forgive them. I paid their debt."

172

Where is the Lamb?   *September 23*

At the very beginning of the history of the Israelites, when
Abraham offered the sacrifice of his own son, Isaac, not knowing that he was to be the victim, asked his father, "Where is
the lamb?" The father said, "God will provide." That question rang through the centuries. And at Passover every family offered a lamb, shed its blood. But where is the lamb?
When John the Baptist was preaching beyond the Jordan,
when about two million pilgrims would be starting their way
up to Jerusalem, crossing the Jordan and going from Jericho
up to the great city, he saw families leading this one-year-old
lamb. It had a blue or scarlet ribbon around the neck and
was often led by the children. But in the crowd he saw someone, and he said, "Look! The Lamb of God, who takes away
the sin of the world." The question of Isaac had been answered. Where is the lamb? The Lamb is on the altar; the
Lamb is in heaven; the Lamb is in the center of the Church;
the Lamb feeds the nations, says the book of Revelation.

Wash one another's feet   *September 24*

I have always wondered why St. John said absolutely nothing
about the Eucharist in his gospel. He has the washing of the
feet; he has the Last Supper in great detail, but not the institution. Why not? Because John was writing at the end of
the century. Remember that St. Paul had considerable trouble with the church at Corinth. One of the troubles there
was that the rich people ate at home. And the poor came,
and there was little for them to eat outside of the broken,
divine bread which they received. St. John wanted to em-
phasize that the Eucharist is not only a personal communion
of the soul with Christ; it is, rather, the fact that we are one
body and that we are bound to service to the whole Church

and to the whole world. If, then, St. Paul complained about the eating of the meal rather selfishly, John the evangelist saw the need of reminding us, "No, the Eucharist is related to the poor." The foundation of our commitment to the world is the holy Eucharist. This is our body. And therefore John reminds us that Jesus said, "You call me Lord, and indeed I am. But if I wash your feet, then wash one another's." Feed the world.

Real power comes from Christ September 25

We can be surrounded with instruments of power and still be ineffective, like Gehazi. When Elisha told Gehazi to go and raise to life the dead boy—which the prophet did later on—he gave him his wand or walking cane. Gehazi could do nothing with it, because he was unable to communicate power through it. So it is with radio; so it is with television; so it is with the pulpit; so it is with the press. Unless there is something in us, unless Christ is in us, and Christ comes out, we are just as ineffective as Gehazi. We are very much interested in using the media, and rightly so. But believe me, unless there is the spirit of Christ infusing the Gehazis, they will never get the boy off the bed.

Unconscious good influence September 26

There are some people who are good influences. And they are unconscious. We do not always know what they are. There was a Protestant woman in France who was converted by a bishop who had given a sermon on the Blessed Sacrament. She hid in church and found later on that evening that the bishop came back to make a visit to the Blessed Sacrament. She asked to take instructions. His shadow fell upon her, as Peter's did on the sick people. He was genuine; he was true.

Casting shadows

We are always casting shadows. Mother Teresa came to New York to one of her houses, which was on one of the worst streets in the city. The street itself was covered with litter, dirt, filth, garbage, and paper. This tiny little woman got a broom and went out to sweep. And the women on the other side of the street, who had thrown out all this garbage, got their brooms and came down. Mother Teresa never asked them to do it. Somehow or other, Christ was in her. So it was with the influence of Pope John XXIII. Everyone who came into contact with him felt the presence of Christ. There was none of that curial politeness. It was a genuine holiness that broke through so that he could even influence Khrushchev and others.

Noah's ark

The Church is like Noah's ark that was full of both clean and unclean animals. It must have had an unholy smell, and yet it was carrying eight persons to salvation. The world today is tearing up the photographs of a good society, a good family, a happy, individual personal life. But the Church is keeping the negatives. And when the moment comes when the world wants a reprint, we will have them.

A foretaste of judgment

Once when I was waiting outside for an audience with Pope Pius XII, I was troubled in spirit. I was saying to myself, the good Lord has given me many more opportunities than he's given to other priests: education and opportunities for apostolate, and how little I have done with them. I was disconsolate. Then when I went in and saw Pope Pius XII, I said,

"Your Holiness, I have just discovered how easy judgment is going to be."

He said, "Tell me, I would like to know."

I said, "Well, I was just saying to myself how much I've failed, how little I have loved the Church, really. Then I come in here, and I find the Church personalized. You are the Church, and I am deeply moved at seeing you and how much I love you. I think that's just the way it's going to be when we go before the face of our dear Lord. We will be discontented with ourselves, but when we go there, we will be surprised how much we really have loved him."

"Yes," he said, "that's exactly the way it will be."

Who can open the scroll   *September 30*

It is hard for us to understand the history of the Church. We all know it. We have asked ourselves a thousand questions. Why should the faith in China be snuffed out? Why should we have had in the last fifty years more martyrs than the Church had in the first 300? Why was there such a persecution in Ireland, where there was obedience and loyalty to the Church? Contemporary history puzzles us. It puzzled John. The whole history of the world was summed up in that scroll of which John wrote in the book of Revelation: "Who can open that book with the seven seals?" We would know the answer to every detail of human history. John tells his concern about it: "And then I saw in the right hand of the one who sat on the throne, a scroll with writing inside and out. And it was sealed up with seven seals, and I saw a mighty angel proclaiming in a loud voice: Who is worthy to open the scroll and to break its seal?" Yes, who can open it? Who can understand history? "There was no one in heaven or on earth or under the earth able to open the scroll or to look inside it. I was in tears because no one was found worthy to open the book and to look inside. But one of the elders said: Do not weep, for the Lion from the tribe of Judah, the scion of David, has won the right to open the scroll and break its seven seals. And then I saw standing in the very middle of the throne, inside the circle of living creatures and the circle of the elders a Lamb with the marks of slaughter upon him. And the Lamb went and took the scroll from the right hand of the one who sat on the throne, and when he took it the four living creatures and the twenty-four elders fell down before the Lamb. And each of the elders had a harp and they held the golden bowls of incense and the prayers of God's people and they were singing a song: Thou art worthy to take the scroll and to break the seals for thou wast slain and by thy blood thou didst purchase for God men of every tribe and language and people and nation. Thou hast made of them a royal house to serve God as priests and they shall reign upon the earth." It is only the cross, only Christ crucified, only the Lamb with the marks of slaughter upon him who is able to open the book.

October

Christ stands at the right hand of the Father   *October 1*

The understanding of human history is at the cross. That's why the Vatican Council told us that the whole spiritual life of the Church is summed up in the Eucharist: in the sacrifice, in the sacrament, in the Lamb of God. We will have to wait for the reading of that scroll. In the meantime, heaven is responsive to what happens on earth. Heaven is responsive, certainly, to what is happening to the Church in each part of the western world and all over the world. As a matter of fact, when, for example, St. Paul [then Saul] began to persecute the church of Damascus, as the church in Warsaw might be persecuted today, the heavens were opened and the Lamb spoke. "Why are you persecuting me?" Not in the past tense, but the present. It was Christ standing at the right hand of the Father. We say in the Apostles' Creed, "He sits at the right hand of the Father." When the Church is persecuted, Christ stands at the right hand of the Father. For the sake of the Church in the eastern part of the world and in Asia, he's standing. See how responsive heaven is to what happens to the Church? When Stephen was stoned, he, too, saw the heavens opened and Christ standing at the right hand of the Father.

Only one Church   *October 2*

Who is it that ever started the idea that there are two kinds of church, institutional and charismatic? You can't have a body without a soul. You can't have a soul without a body. There is only one Church, and that is the body of Christ. And as Christ is living in his Church, we listen to him, and we become attentive to him. We are not rebellious against him. We love him when he speaks through Peter. As G. K. Chesterton said, "I'd rather we had a pontiff that is right when the world is wrong, not so much one that is right when the world is right." When the world is wrong, we have a guide. That is a great consolation.

The source of inner strength   *October 3*

I once gave a day of recollection for Mother Teresa's group in New York, and I talked to the pastor, who was one of the wisest men, when it came to social work, that I ever talked to in my life. He'd been there in that locality twenty-nine years, where seventy or eighty percent of the buildings were vacant and burnt-out. I asked him, "What is your experience during these last ten or fifteen years?"

"Well," he said, "we had a number of priests and sisters who just flooded our area. They were going to reform everything. They had to be involved. They'd been reading Harvey Cox, not Mark or Luke. They ran up against frustrations. Their theories didn't work out." Their idealism was defeated. They could not drive out any devils. And because they had no interior strength, they all left. "If", he said, "they had had interior strength, if they loved Christ and the cross and the Blessed Sacrament, they could have taken it, as I have taken it and as I love it." There is no point then in holding workshops to discuss one or the other point of view, because the two must be put together.

Mary and the Good Samaritan   *October 4*

The Gospel of Luke, that wonderful evangelist who was so human—the scribe of the meekness of Christ, as he has been called—tells the story of the Good Samaritan. Immediately afterward, he tells the story of Martha and Mary. In other words, you love the story of the Good Samaritan and you're going out on the highways, are you? You're going to care for all these wounded people that you pick up, and you're going to take them to a hospice? Try, but read on. Do not become too busy, otherwise you might be like Martha, preparing a thousand-island salad, gathering the salad from each of the thousand islands. You have to take time out to be like Mary and sit at the feet of Christ. This is the truth. Too often we have presented this as the conflict between age groups, of young and old. It is not a conflict of age groups any more than it was on the Mount of Transfiguration. We cannot always remain on the mountain. We have to go down into the valley. There is the ecstasy, but there also are the problems. The two have to be kept together.

Conversion without a word   *October 5*

I once asked Mother Teresa how she converted 15,000 men out of the gutters of Calcutta. "How, after dragging these poor mortals into your hospice could you ever evangelize them and teach them the gospel?"

"Well," she said, "I didn't. When I took care of them and showed them love, I would say to them, 'Would you like to hear about Christ?' And they would say, 'Is Christ like you? Is Christ like you?' 'No,' I would say, 'but I try to be like him.' 'Then I want to be a Christian.'" It was that simple. That is the way we should act. So that the world will, without ever hearing a word from us, know about us and what we stand for.

How we will be real Christians   *October 6*

When we stay close to the good Lord in the Blessed Sacrament, we will see the flesh of all the poor people that we meet as an extension of the body of Christ. That outlook will come through to them. Then we will be Christians. Then we will not be in the mountain in ecstasy nor in the valley, impotent and ineffective. But we will be the kind of Christians the world is looking for.

A group of Russian soldiers broke into a barn not very long ago in Russia and found hundreds of people in prayer. They said to them, "You are violating the Soviet law. Prayer is forbidden. We give you five minutes to leave. All who remain will be shot." Two left. The Russian soldiers threw down their guns and said, "We want to be Christians too. We only wanted to be sure that you were really Christians."

Only by the sacrifice of Christ   *October 7*

The sons of Aaron, two young priests, had just been ordained, and they came into the tabernacle where there was the altar of sacrifice, the altar of incense beyond, the golden candlestick, and the bread of perpetual presence. The two sons lit the fires of the altar of intercession with a strange fire, says the scripture, for which they were struck dead by God. And Aaron did not move. He knew the justice of God's judgment, and Moses said, "Remove the bodies." They went on with the liturgy. Why were these newly ordained priests struck dead? Because the fires of the altar of intercession must be lighted from the altar of sacrifice. There is no intercession except through sacrifice, and they skipped Calvary, as it were, and thought that heaven would be opened and their intercession to God accepted without a sacrifice. See how strict and severe God is in driving home this truth to us about the death and sacrifice of Christ.

What do we want? *October 8*

We want life; we want truth; we want love: these are our basic needs. Not life for five more minutes, not the truths of geography to the exclusion of history, and not a love of society; we want a life without end, total truth, perfect love. And, we might ask, from where do the rays of sunshine in a chapel come? Not from under the pews; for the source, we must go to pure light. So for the source of life and truth and love, we have to go to the Father who is life itself, to the Son who is the Word and truth, and to the Holy Spirit who is love. God, therefore, is life and truth and love—everything that we want on earth in its fullness—each dwelling in the other and fully one in being.

The Father and the Son are both eternal *October 9*

The Father thinks, but he does not think as we do. We have a succession of thoughts. The Father has only one thought. One word that reaches to the abyss of all things that are known and can be known. Where did that thought of God come from? He generated it. Just as we generated the thought of triangularity. We have never seen justice out for a walk. We do not know the latitude of fortitude. So God generated a thought, as we generate thoughts, except that his was one that contains all knowledge. Because he generated it, that thought, that Word is called a Son. One did not preexist the other. A little child came home from catechism to an unbelieving father. "What did you learn in catechism today?"

"That there are three Persons in God—Father, Son, and Holy Spirit—and they are all eternal."

The father said, "Don't be stupid. I am your father, you are my son. I existed a long time before you did."

The little boy said, "No, you didn't. You didn't begin to be a father, until I began to be a son."

The Church is the body of Christ *October 10*

The Church is a body; it is the body of Christ. He took a new body. For his physical body he now uses a social body, an ecclesial body. Just as my own body is made up of millions and millions of cells and vivified by one soul, governed by a visible head, and presided over by an invisible mind, so too all of us who have in any way become incorporated to Christ are the cells in his body. We are one, because we are vivified by one soul, which is the Holy Spirit; we are presided over by the invisible head, Christ in heaven, who is the head of the body, and we are governed by the visible head, our Holy Father. That is the Church. At the Vatican Council, we defined the Church as the mystery, and that's what it is. It is the great sacrament of sacraments because it has something physical about it and something invisible about it.

The gift and the gifts *October 11*

Now there are gifts. They are called charisms, sometimes. There are many of them. St. Paul mentions about fifteen. What is the difference between the gift and the charisms? In theology we make a distinction between *gratia gratum faciens* and *gratia gratis data*. *Gratia gratum faciens* is that which makes us pleasing to God. That is the gift, that is grace. *Gratia gratis data* is the charism. Preaching is one charism. Would you believe that administration is another? What is the difference between the gift and the charism? The gift makes us pleasing to God, and the charism makes us helpful in relationship to others. *To others*: that is the point. For example, I have the charism of preaching. People think I am holy. I talk about holy things. So they say, "He must be a holy priest." Not necessarily. There are some who worked miracles in the Old Testament that were not too holy. That's another one of the charisms. If there is any holiness in me, it is not because I exercise that particular charism. As a matter of fact, I know a hundred actors who could do better than I am doing. If there is to be any holiness, it has to be before I come into the pulpit and after I leave it. There I am just exercising a gift that God gave. And he could take it away.

Building up the Church   *October 12*

Gifts can be transient things. That's why St. Paul says of several of them, "They will pass." See how Saul lost his gift, or Samson. Samson had the charism of strength. And Samson one day said, "I will go out and do as I've done before", and scripture says that "he knew not that the Lord had left him." He no longer had the charism. So these particular gifts can be lost. We therefore have to keep a due balance in the Church, and not be overemphatic about certain gifts, not forming elites, not allowing anyone to say, "We have a monopoly on the Spirit. You join our group. I am of Paul; I am of Cephas; I am of Apollos." The test is always: does it build up the Church? If it does not build up the Church, then it is not properly used.

The law of withdrawal and return   *October 13*

There is such a thing in the order of the world and in the order of the Spirit as the law of withdrawal and return. We never become strong in one area unless we have prepared for it with a withdrawal and retirement. When St. Paul, for example, met Christ, he went into Arabia for three years. He, this Pharisee of Pharisees, this strong Jew, came out of Arabia, and said, "There is neither Jew nor Greek, there is neither slave nor free." That withdrawal made him a different man when he returned. Julius Caesar went to Gaul for eight years—the withdrawal—then came back eight years later and crossed the Rubicon and saved Rome. Our Blessed Lord was thirty years obeying, three years teaching, three hours redeeming. And the spiritual life is conditioned upon that. This idea of saying that we are too busy to do anything else, to pray or make a holy hour, means that we are not doing well. There is no withdrawal, no gathering of forces. Athletic contests have moments of respite. So in the military, momentary retreat can make for a strong offensive. So we have to withdraw spiritually if we are ever to be strong.

The Spirit works in two hearts   *October 14*

Douglas Hyde, who was editor of the communist *Daily Worker*, told me that he and his wife (who was co-editor) were one night listening to the Soviet foreign minister, Litvinov, on British wireless. Suddenly she got up, shut off the wireless, and said, "I don't think he wants peace. I think he wants war. He's just talking peace."

Her husband said, "Don't talk that way. You're not talking like a communist."

She said, "I don't care what I'm talking like, but I don't think he wants peace."

"If you continue to talk that way," he said, "I will report you to the party and you will be disciplined."

"Report me; I don't care", she said.

"Do you know what you're talking like?" he said. "You're talking as if you might become a Catholic."

She said, "I am."

He said, "So am I." Here were two people editing a communist newspaper and the Holy Spirit worked on them separately and changed them until they were both brought into the Church.

The denial of guilt   *October 15*

We are living in the only period of the world's history in which there is a universal denial of guilt. Dostoevsky wrote: "The time is coming when men will say there is no sin; there is no guilt; there is only hunger. And they will come crying and fawning to our feet saying, 'Give us bread.' " It used to be that Catholics were the only ones who believed in the Immaculate Conception. Now everybody believes that he was immaculately conceived.

Can children understand sin?   *October 16*

In the last few years we have had the idea that children should not be taught about sin and that confession should not be required before communion because it would give children a wrong sense of guilt. However, every child three years of age and older understands the meaning of a broken relationship, which is the essence of sin. Just let a mother tell a young child, "Mommy no longer loves you", and you will see the disturbance caused by a broken relationship.

Psychiatry and sin   *October 17*

So general has the denial of sin been, that it has not been theologians who have resurrected the idea, but psychiatrists.

Karl Menninger, of the Menninger Psychiatric Institute of Kansas, has published a book entitled *What Ever Became of Sin*. He shows the slow devolution of the concept of sin. According to him, moralists stopped preaching about sin because everything was love; then the jurists picked the theme, and sin under law became a crime. Then the psychiatrists took it up from the legalists, and sin then became a symptom or a complex. Some rather tragic effects have resulted from this denial of sin. First of all, we have many complexes that are produced by sin, and we are blind to the true cause, which is guilt.

Guilt and neurosis   *October 18*

Some people have developed psychiatric problems from an excess of guilt. But an abnormal show of guilt does not prove that there is no normal guilt at the basis and foundation. A woman once came to see me about her brother. She told me he had been under psychiatric help for three years and had wasted away to about one hundred pounds.

He looked almost like a ghost when he came to see me. He was so thin. I asked him to talk to me for about forty-five minutes and promised not to interrupt him. At the end of forty-five minutes I asked him, "How much did you steal?"

He replied, "I didn't steal anything."

I persisted, "How much did you steal?"

"I didn't tell you I stole."

"How much was it?"

He gave in and confessed, "Three thousand dollars. How did you know I stole?"

I replied, "You told me that you always wiped off whatever money you put into the collection box. I thought perhaps you were involved with dirty money." Three years of psychiatric treatment had failed to uncover the real problem, guilt, resulting from thievery.

The sin of King David   *October 19*

Today we have become patients instead of penitents. We have rationalized our guilt to the extent that it hardly makes sense anymore to ask anyone, "Why did you do it?" The answer will be a mere rationalization. Remember the story of David. He was out on his sundeck one day when he saw Bathsheba in the opposite apartment. He invited her over to see his etchings. She became pregnant with his child. Bathsheba's husband, Uriah, was at war, so David sent for him and told him to go home to his wife. That way he could transfer paternity to the husband. But Uriah replied, "I can't go home to my wife. We are at war." So David got him drunk, but he still didn't go home; he slept in David's front yard. Then David sent Uriah back to battle and said to the general, "Some are killed in battle. Maybe Uriah will be killed." Of course Uriah was killed. David had no sense of guilt whatever until Nathan came to him one day with a social problem. He talked about a poor man who had one ewe lamb. The neighbor, a rich neighbor, killed that ewe lamb to serve his friends. And David said, "That man shall restore fourfold and pay with his life." Nathan replied, "Thou art the man. You stole the ewe lamb of Uriah." Then David wrote Psalm 51, and his guilt came out.

Forgiveness and the blood   *October 20*

How is sin forgiven? What is the ultimate basis for the remission of sin? The answer is given in Hebrews 9:27: "Without the shedding of blood there is no forgiveness of sin." This is an absolute. Why is it necessary to shed blood? Because sin is in the blood. It is in the blood of the degenerate, in the blood of the alcoholic, in the blood of the addict. Sin is in the blood of the diseased. It is running through every gateway and alley of the body, and it would seem that to expunge sin, we would have to get rid of blood. Perhaps that is one reason. Another reason, as we read in the book of Leviticus, is that the life of man is in the blood. The higher the life, the more precious the blood. When you come to the life of Christ, who sheds his blood, you get the total remission of sin.

Behold the Lamb of God   *October 21*

As John was preaching his hard message of penance and laying the axe to the root of the tree, he saw all the lambs being brought to Jerusalem for the Passover sacrifice. Josephus tells us that ten or fifteen years after the death of Christ, 260,000 lambs were offered in the temple in Jerusalem. The religion of Israel was a veritable hemorrhage of blood. As John watched this procession of the Passover, Isaac's question was still in the air, "Where is the lamb for the sacrifice? Where is the lamb?" Suddenly John stopped and looked out at someone in the crowd, interrupted his discourse, and said, "Look, look, the Lamb of God, who takes away the sin of the world."

Heaven was opened by Christ's blood   *October 22*

In the temple at the time of our Lord, the veil was about sixty feet high. This great veil was sprinkled with blood by the high priest on the Day of Atonement. He alone could enter on this day and commune with divinity. When he sprinkled the blood, it gave him the right to go behind the veil. On the hill of Calvary, on that great Passover, other blood was being sprinkled. At the moment that the lance was run into the side of our Blessed Lord, this veil of the temple was rent, not from bottom to top, for a man could do that, but rent from top to bottom. The holy of holies, which the people were never allowed to see (except for the high priest on the Day of Atonement) was opened. This was merely the earthly counterpart of something else that was opened on the hill of Calvary. A mystery beautifully described in the epistle to the Hebrews: "So now my friends, the blood of Jesus makes us free to enter boldly into the sanctuary by the new living way which he has opened for us through the curtain, the way of his flesh." So there were two curtains, the curtain in the temple in Jerusalem, and the curtain of the flesh on Mount Calvary. The holy of holies, which was only a symbol, was opened and revealed to human eyes. The holy of holies, the heart of Christ, was opened on the hill of Calvary. So the blood of Christ makes us free to enter the sanctuary by the new living way which he has opened through the curtain of his flesh. Heaven was opened by that act.

The worst thing in the world   October 23

Sin is not the worst thing in the world. The worst thing in the world is the denial of sin. If I am blind and deny that there is any such thing as light, shall I ever see? If I am deaf and deny that there is any such thing as harmony, will I ever hear? If I deny that there is any such thing as sin, how shall I ever be forgiven? The denial of sin is the unforgivable sin, for it makes redemption impossible. So even our sins, when we bring them to the blood of Christ, sometimes have a good side. We are washed in that blood, and we rejoice and thank the Lord; for if we had never sinned, we never could call Jesus "Savior".

The Church's real problem

We have been surfeited in America in the last few years with
sociological, psychological, and theological surveys of what
has happened to the Church. But they are not of much avail
because cultural reasons do not explain what has happened.
The Church has undergone a great crisis and some degen-
eration in every country in the world: Africa is suffering; the
church in Asia is suffering; Europe is suffering. If there were
only cultural reasons, the effect would not be so universal. It
can only be, therefore, that there are some other causes besides the cultural and national at work. One that is not to be
neglected is the demonic. Whenever there is an outpouring
of the Holy Spirit, there is always a strong effort put forth by
the diabolic. For example, when Moses worked miracles,
the magicians of the Pharoahs duplicated some of them.
When the Church received the Holy Spirit, there was the
persecution of Stephen. With the Vatican Council, there has
been an outpouring of the Holy Spirit and also an outpouring of the evil spirit. But our theologians have neglected the
demonic. God says, "I am who am." The devil said, "I am
who am not." The demonic is always most powerful when
he is denied. It is almost impossible today to find a theologian writing about the demonic, unless it be to deny it. That
is not true of literature. It is not true of psychiatry. It is true
only of theology.

The demonic is contempt of the cross

What is the demonic from the biblical point of view? It is
contempt of the cross. Let us go back to the meeting our
Lord held in the half-pagan, half-Jewish city of Caesarea Phil-
ippi. Our Lord then asked the most important question that
can be asked of anyone. Finally, when Peter had given the

answer, "Thou art the Christ, the Son of the living God", our Lord immediately said, "I must go up to Jerusalem to be crucified to be delivered over to the Gentiles and the third day rise again." As soon as the Lord had said that, Peter laid hold of his arm and said, "This shall not be." I am willing to have a divine Christ but I am not willing to have a suffering Christ. Our Lord said, "Get behind me, Satan." Do not try to lead me. I lead you. Our Lord called Peter Satan. Why was he Satan? Because he was tempting our Lord from the cross.

The temptations of Christ   *October 26*

At the beginning of our Lord's public life, he was led by the Spirit to meet the evil spirit. There are three temptations described in the gospels. I will translate them into modern language. Satan was offering our Lord three shortcuts from the cross. Satan was saying, "You are here to establish your kingdom; you want to win over the hearts of men. I will give you the secret."

The first temptation was to escape from the cross: allow people to follow their *id*. "Look at those stones down there. They look like loaves of bread. You have not eaten in forty days; you have a hunger instinct. Others have a sex instinct, or a power instinct. They have got an ego instinct. You want to win men; let them follow their drives. Obey the *id*. Then they will follow you. But not the cross."

The second temptation of Satan was technological. Satan was saying, "People love wonders, miracles, marvels, anything that makes them say, 'Oh!' They will not remember the marvels very long, but give them new wonders. Throw yourself down from the steeple; fly to the moon. They'll not remember your name in three weeks. Give them another wonder. Change nature. Overcome it. Give them a pill. But not a cross."

The third temptation was political. As if holding the whole earth like a shiny globe in his hands, Satan said to our Lord, "All these kingdoms are mine. They're mine." Was Satan telling the truth for once in his life? Here he suggested to the Lord that theology is politics. "Forget you are God; you are the Messiah. The mastery of the world and the future will depend entirely on politics. So go into the political arena, and I can help you, for all these kingdoms are mine. But forget about the cross."

Satan tried to tempt our Blessed Lord from the cross. This is the essence of the demonic.

The accuser and the defender   *October 27*

Before we sin, Satan is always our defender, and Christ is the accuser. Satan is the defender: "Sure, the Vatican Council changed all that. We don't believe that any more; do you? After all, you've got to be up-to-date." Christ seems to be saying, "Choose either me or the world. I pray not for the world." Then after we sin, what is Satan called in the book of Revelation? The accuser. That's what he is in the book of Job and in Zechariah. "Now see what you've done. No hope, you might just as well go all the way." And Christ is now the defender "Come to me, all ye who labor." "Though your sins be as scarlet, they shall be made white as snow."

The two faces   *October 28*

Each and every one of us, at the end of the journey of life, will come face to face with either one or the other of two faces: either the merciful face of Christ or the miserable face of Satan. We can journey down a thousand times ten thousand roads, but we will end at either one of those two faces. And one of them, either the merciful face of Christ or the miserable face of Satan, will say, "Mine, mine." May we be Christ's.

The effect of a minor incident

In Yugoslavia some years ago a young boy was serving Mass, and he dropped the cruet. The priest slapped him, and said, "Get out and never come back." He never came back. He became the communist leader of Yugoslavia, Tito. If that priest had ever come to the good Lord in order to review what he had done, there would have been, perhaps, some remission and an altering of the effect.

I can remember when I was a boy serving at the cathedral under Bishop John L. Spalding. I was about seven years of age, and I dropped the wine cruet at the offertory. Now let me tell you that there is no atomic explosion which can equal in intensity the sound of a cruet falling on a marble floor. I was frightened to death because we altar boys thought he was a stern man. After Mass, he said, "Come here, young man. Where are you going to school when you get big?" To a seven-year-old, big is high school. I said, "Spalding Institute". That was the high school named after him, a much more diplomatic answer than I thought at the time.

He said, "I said when you get big. Did you ever hear of Louvain?"

I said, "No."

"Well, you go home and tell your mother that I said that when you got big, you were to go to the University of Louvain, and some day you will be just as I am."

So I went home and told my mother what he had said, and she said, "Yes, that's a great university in Europe." I never once thought of that incident until I had been ordained two years and stepped off a train in Louvain. I said, "Oh, this is where Bishop Spalding told me to go." It was an event that in some way altered my life as it altered the life of Tito in the opposite way.

How one thief was caught   *October 30*

After I had been preaching on Good Friday at St. Patrick's one year, a woman came back to the main altar, her hair disheveled, a haunted look on her face, and cursed me violently. I said, "Why did you come in here?"

She said, "To steal purses."

I said, "Did you get any?"

"No," she said, "that second word of yours got me—the word to the good thief." Then she said, "Why am I talking to you, you blankety-blank? You'll just tell the cops."

I said, "Why do the cops want you?" She pulled out clippings from the Los Angeles Times and FBI folders. Three of her confreres were in San Quentin, and the FBI was looking for her. I asked her if she had ever been a Catholic, and she said yes, she had, up until the age of fourteen. So I heard her confession, and she became a daily communicant. But she was unable to work. I supported her for about twenty years until she died. Well, I was harboring a criminal, so after some time I said to her, "I must make known to the FBI that I know about you." She agreed, and I told the FBI. I said, "You're looking for a woman."

"Do we want her badly?" they said.

I said, "Oh, yes. Her name is so-and-so. She's a daily communicant at St. Patrick's."

They said, "You have done far more for her than we or the prisons could have done, so we're letting her go." So this chance incident of coming in to a church on Good Friday to steal purses made all the difference.

When we bring the crosses, the handicaps, that we have in our life into the prayer of the holy hour, we will begin to see that God is talking to us. Not only does he talk to us in events, but here we have a beautiful opportunity to distinguish between acceptance and rebellion in the face of all of the trials of life. Acceptance: "Thy will be done." Rebellion: "Why did this happen to me?" The two thieves on either side of our Blessed Lord are perfect examples of these two attitudes.

November

Let us be sent

Now we have many disappointments in life, and they are all fuel for abandonment to the will of God. In the Church today, we are losing the sense of mission. We are no longer sent. The Father sent the Son, the Son sent the apostles, the apostles sent us. We don't want to be sent; we want to choose where we go. We want our options. So we can never be very sure that we are doing God's will. We are sure that we are doing our own, and, generally, when we get what we want, we don't like it. Please God, we'll soon ask him, "Lord, what do you want me to do? Just tell me."

How I learned to obey

I spent two years in graduate work in Washington after I was ordained, and then I was abroad for about five years. When I was done, I sent my bishop two letters. One letter invited me to start a school of scholastic philosophy at Columbia University. The second letter invited me to go to Oxford with Father Ronald Knox to open the first Catholic college at Oxford since the Reformation. I sent them to my bishop, and I said, "Which shall I accept?" He said, "Come home." He sent me to the worst parish in the diocese as a curate. It was the off-scouring of the earth. Only twenty percent of the parish could speak English. None of the streets was paved. And I said, "All right, this is it. This is what the Lord wants me to do." I was perfectly satisfied. After about a year, the bishop phoned me and said, "You're to go to Washington to Catholic University as a professor. I promised them you would three years ago."

I said, "Why didn't you let me go when I came home?"

He said, "I just wanted to find out whether or not you would be obedient. Now run along." So I've been running along ever since.

Prayer and worship   *November 3*

It is not our will that matters; it is the Lord's. This is the difference between prayer and worship. Prayer is the expression of my will; worship is the acceptance of God's will. The two are quite distinct. Just run through the Old Testament and see how very often, for example, one of the great biblical characters, like Abraham, prays to God, expresses his own will, and then God says to him, "Offer your son, Isaac." And he prostrates himself. That's his worship.

Another beautiful instance is David's response to his son's death. As we read in 2 Samuel, after Nathan told him that he had killed Uriah: "The Lord struck the boy whom Uriah's wife had borne to David. And he was very ill. David prayed to God for the child; he fasted and went in and spent the night fasting, lying on the ground. The older men of the household tried to get him to rise from the ground, but he refused and would eat no food with them. On the seventh day the boy died, and David's servants were afraid to tell him. 'While the boy was alive,' they said, 'we spoke to him and he did not listen to us; how can we now tell him that the boy is dead? He may do something desperate.' David saw his servants whispering among themselves and guessed that the boy was dead. He asked, 'Is the boy dead?' And they answered, 'He is dead.' Then David rose from the ground, washed and anointed himself, and put on fresh clothes; he entered the house of the Lord and prostrated himself there. Then he went home, asked for food to be brought, and when it was ready, he ate. The servants asked him, 'What is this? While the boy lived you fasted and wept for him, but now that he is dead you rise up and eat?' He answered, 'While the boy was still alive I fasted and wept, thinking, "It may be that the Lord would be gracious to me, and the boy may live." But now that he is dead, why should I fast? Can I bring him back? I shall go to him, and he will not come back to me.' "

David worshiped the Lord. The difference between praying and worshiping is the difference between my will and God's will.

We get less than we deserve   *November 4*

It very often happens that when we have a little opportunity to do our own will, we can become much closer to the Lord by accepting his. In the book of the prophet Ezra, we read something that we need to dwell on very often. Ezra says: "We have suffered for our evil deeds and for our great guilt— although our God has punished us less than our iniquities deserve." Indeed, if we are honest, we will admit that we all receive fewer blows than we deserve.

Transferability of merit   *November 5*

In the holy hour, therefore, we will begin the work of transferability of merits. Because as we live in a mystical body, the merits of one can be transferred to another. The believing wife, says St. Paul, sanctifies the unbelieving husband. The believing husband sanctifies the unbelieving wife. No man lives for himself, says Paul, and no man dies for himself. There is this transfer of the faith, as it were, of the wife to the husband and vice versa. If we burn our face, doctors will graft skin from another part of the body to the face. If we are suffering from anemia, doctors will transfuse blood from another member of society to us to cure us of that anemic condition. If it is possible to transfuse blood, it is possible to transfuse sacrifice. If it is possible to graft skin, it is also possible to graft prayer. In the holy hour, our prayers, our petitions, our adoration will be transferred to our brothers and sisters in Christ.

On the cross or under it? *November 6*

We learn this great mystery before the eucharistic Lord: to think of our prayer life as embracing all the circumstances and details of life, interpreting them in that hour. I believe that every single person in the world in his heart is either on the cross or underneath it. On the cross with Christ—"I am crucified with Christ", says Paul. Those of us who are suffering are more physically on the cross. The Blessed Mother and St. John and the women at the foot of the cross were on the cross by sympathy. So everyone in the world is either on the cross by recognizing the merits of Christ and by sharing that cross, or else under the cross. And many of the faithful today are under it, saying, "Come down, come down and we will believe." There is a new disease creeping into the Church, *staurophobia*. *Stauros* in Greek is "cross", and *phobia*, "fear": staurophobia, fear of the cross. Anything but discipline. The holy hour, therefore, will train you in abandonment and resignation, in acceptance of God's will and in utilizing all of the actions of the day. For on the last day the Lord will say, "Show me your hands." And we will have to have the scars as he had them. And once we take that one scar of the hour and give it to him every day, then we can be sure that he will say to us, "Come, beloved of my Father in heaven."

Energy   *November 7*

Why does our energy decline? There are two theories about energy. One is that we have just a certain amount of it, like money in the bank. When it's spent, we are exhausted. The other theory is that there's a blockage of the energy, and energy itself can be renewed. As a matter of fact, we never get the second wind until we have used up the first. We never enjoy the swim until after the shock of the first cold plunge. Hypnotists have shown that by suggesting to a man that he is strong, he can lift a weight sixty percent greater than normal. If it is suggested to him by hypnotism that he is weak, he can lift forty percent less than normal. I think the secret of all energy is that as sanctity declines, energy declines. When love of Christ begins to lessen, then we lose energy. The remedy to not having time is wasting some time. Waste some time for Christ's sake.

Water from the well of Bethlehem   *November 8*

One example of wasting time was that of the woman who came into Simon's house. She broke the vessel, not calculating less or more, and she expressed the sheer ecstasy of giving, not holding back. That kind of foolishness was praised by the Lord. Another remarkable instance is from the Old Testament. David had gone back to his own native town of Bethlehem. Like every man who returns to his early home, he must have had a nostalgia for tastes and smells and scenes. What David yearned for was water from the well of Bethlehem. As the Holy Spirit tells the story in 1 Chronicles 11:15–19, "David was in the stronghold and a Philistine garrison held

Bethlehem. A longing came over David, and he exclaimed, 'If only I could have a drink of water from the well by the gate of Bethlehem!' " At this, three strong men made their way through the Philistine lines, drew water from the well by the gate of Bethlehem, and brought it to David. Now what did David do with it? "David refused to drink it; he poured it out to the Lord and said, 'God forbid that I should do such a thing! Can I drink the blood of these men? They have brought it at the risk of their lives.' " If David had drunk of that water, the holy scripture would not be telling the story. It was something that was too precious to keep for himself.

Being wasteful   *November 9*

When we keep certain things for ourselves, they spoil. We keep flesh too much for ourselves, and it turns into lust. We keep money too much for ourselves, and it turns into avarice. We keep learning too much for ourselves, and it turns into conceit. We keep time too much for ourselves, and we waste our lives. I wonder if at the end of our days the slow process of just wasting away is not due to the way we live during our life. Have we been sufficiently wasteful of the gifts that God has given to us, whatever they happen to be, particularly time? Just think of how much time you waste in the course of a day; over a daily newspaper, when the only things you can be absolutely sure are true are the sporting page and the stock market indexes. (If, for example, the Redskins beat the Rams, you don't say, "This is a Republican paper, I'll go out and see what a Democratic paper has to say.") We waste time on useless reading and then say, "I don't have time for an hour of prayer." Actually, we do not have time for anything else. When this hour is wasted before the Lord, then it will be remembered like the water from the well of Bethlehem. There must be in our lives a kind of impulsiveness, a giving that doesn't measure. Perhaps we reckon our lives and our time and our energy just a little too mathematically.

Walking on water   *November 10*

After Jesus had multiplied the loaves and the fishes at Capernaum, the apostles were caught up in the glow of all his acclaim. It was wonderful for the apostles to see our Lord acclaimed as king and as prophet. Because the apostles were caught up in this enthusiasm, the Lord says, get over to the other side of the lake. He didn't want them to be spoiled. They start rowing across the lake, and our Lord goes up the mountaintop. The night passes, there's a storm, with fog and rain. It was three o'clock in the morning, and the apostles were rowing against the wind and were frightened. The Lord watched them all the time. Finally, he came toward them, walking on the water. They did not recognize him.

They thought he was a specter, a ghost. And Mark tells us the reason: they did not understand the miracle of the loaves. They did not understand this unseen presence of Christ in the bread of life. And in their fear our Blessed Lord assured them, "Fear not, it is I." Here comes the impulsiveness of a great man, a fool. "Lord, let me walk on the waters." What stupidity—walk on water. Can you imagine what must have gone on in that boat when Peter lifted up his right foot to put it on the water? Thomas must have said to him, "You believe anything, don't you Peter?" But he walked, he really walked on the water. Because the Lord said, "Come, come." Believe the incredible, and you can do the impossible. It is our want of faith that holds us back, even as Peter. Why did he begin to sink? The gospel gives us the reason. He took account of the winds, he began reading some surveys; it was established statistically that 99.44 percent of mankind cannot walk on water. All of the incredulities were in the winds. When he took his eyes off Christ, Peter began to sink.

Pope Paul VI and his namesake   *November 11*

In the last audience that I had with Pope Paul VI, I said, "You're well named, Paul, because you are stoned as Paul was. Stoned by your own, as Paul was stoned when he went from Lystra to Derbe and Antioch in Pisidia." "Yes," he said, "I open my mail at midnight and in almost every letter there is a thorn. And when I lay my head at night on the pillow, I lay it on a crown of thorns. But I cannot tell you what ineffable joy I have in being able to fill up in my poor flesh the sufferings that are wanting, wanting in the Passion of Christ for the sake of his body which is the Church."

Seeing Christ in the sick   *November 12*

When we look at a sick person, or one wounded, or infected, or cancerous, what do we see? If we have developed that vision of seeing Christ in the Eucharist, we will see Christ in the cross of the sick. He is in his faithful people who are consciously offering up all of their sufferings in union with Christ. And we all are edified by certain ones who say, "Well, I offer this up for my sins, for the sake of the Church." Christ is suffering not only in those who have the faith, but he is suffering in those who do not know him, and this is their salvation.

What it means to empty ourselves   *November 13*

To be assumed by the Person of Christ, to act in his name, first of all, we have to empty ourselves. Second, we must be lifted up ourselves. In the second chapter of the letter to the

Philippians, St. Paul says of Christ that the divine nature was his from the first. He did not need to snatch at equality with God, because he was God. He made himself a nothing, assuming the nature of a slave. He made himself a zero. He emptied himself. There was a human nature, but no human person in Christ. There was only the divine Person. That means that in a certain sense we no longer have a human person. Believe me, our spirituality has been ruined by the so-called philosophy of identity. I've got to be me. I've got to do my thing. Since when? Doesn't charity mean doing the other person's thing? Why this affirmation of the ego? Why do we have to act in a certain way to attract the attention of others to our human personality? There's no human personality in us. Christ is in us at all times, acting through us, using us as his instrument.

Between East and West   *November 14*

The western world has very much affirmed the ego of man. That is the great difference between the East and the West. In the eastern world, where there is an overemphasis on the sovereignty of God, God does everything, man does nothing. That is the reason that there's been very little technical progress in the East. In the western world, man does everything, God does nothing. The balance between the two is, "I can do all things in him who strengthens me."

Spend and you will get   *November 15*

In the divine order, we get only when we spend. "Give and it will be given to you." *Date et dabitur*. And when there is this foolishness, then there is a tremendous transformation of heart and soul. One of the great characters of Russian literature, an evil man, Raskolnikov, killed an old woman, not for pleasure, not for money, just simply because there was no distinction between virtue and vice. He admitted his crime to a prostitute named Sonya. One day, he said to Sonya in a fit of anger, "One of three things is going to happen to you. You'll either jump off a bridge; you will go mad; or you will cut your throat." And Sonya picked up the eleventh chapter of John and began reading the resurrection of Lazarus. In other words, there's always an open door, the open door of love.

Foolishness for the Lord   *November 16*

We are busy; we have no spare time. But we have to be fools and spend the time, and then we get back wisdom; and what wisdom there is from communing with the eucharistic Lord. We are captives, captives of his love, captives of his duty. Kindliness to the unlovable people, the projection of the Spirit of Christ to those who would be unforgiving, all this is foolishness. But if you keep up this holy hour, you will be very thankful in your hearts, not just to me, but that the Lord was so good to you.

Christs who don't know it   *November 17*

I have been in mission work for sixteen years and have been in it much longer by affection. I was never very much concerned with the theological problem of what used to be called the salvation of pagans. But traveling around the world and visiting leper colonies and seeing starving people fight vultures in Latin America, seeing starving mothers with starving children strapped to their backs in India, seeing 250,180 people a night sleeping in the street in Calcutta, seeing all of the hunger and want and indigence and pain below the thirtieth parallel, I came to have a new vision of the world.

Traveling through all those worlds, I never saw so many Christs in my life. Christs, yes. But you say, they don't know him. No, they do not consciously know him, but he is in them as long as they do not rebel; he is in them by their sufferings. I was hungry; I was sick; I was naked; I was homeless. When? When? When? No, they didn't know, but Christ was in them. Remember these words were said to the nations, to the Gentiles, and that's how they are saved. We will be surprised to see that many of those who have not known Christ as we have known him may be ahead of us in the kingdom of heaven because they were always with his cross, even though it was unwitting.

Job's question   *November 18*

The Old Testament comes close to an answer for the problem of evil in the book of Job. Here was a wealthy man who was good, and Satan asked God to tempt him. Satan sometimes is the cause of many of the ills of good people. God said: You may touch his flesh, but you may not touch his soul. And poor Job lost all of his flock and all of his children. The only thing that God left him was Mrs. Job, and she said, "Curse God and die." The consolers came, or rather the counselors, three of them. They gave every explanation possible to Job. Job was not satisfied with them; he asked questions: Why was I born? Why was I ever nestled at my mother's breast? Why did I ever see the light of day? Then God appears. Now if God were a Broadway dramatist, he would have answered all the questions of Job and made the answers click. But what does God do? God asks Job questions. "Where were you when I laid the foundations of earth? Upon what are its bases grounded? Who laid the cornerstone? Where is the hiding place of darkness? Out of whose womb came the ice? The frost from heaven, have you engendered it? Can you make the evening star to rise upon the children of men? Can you send forth your voice, and will thunders and lightnings go forth and come back to you and say to you, here we are?" When God finished asking Job questions, Job understood that the questions of God were more satisfying than the answers of men. As a mouse eating piano keys could not understand why anyone should sit at a stool and play Tchaikovsky, so the human mind cannot comprehend God's ways. God did say to Job about the counselors—and let that always be a lesson to them—offer some sacrifices to make up for their stupid answers.

The most often-used word   *November 19*

On a quiz program one day, the question asked, "Which is the most often-used word in the United States?" The answer was "love". It is generally assumed today, thanks to modern ethics, that anything is all right provided that you love. Is it really that simple? There are different forms of love. Unfortunately, we have only one word in English for love. So we have to use it for such disparate expressions as: I love Maryland crabcakes; I love the New York Mets; I love God. That gives you some idea of how confusing the word love is in English.

Greek words for love   *November 20*

The Greeks had three words for love. The first was *eros*. Eros was that little god that used to shoot arrows into the earth to make it fertile. Eros was the subject of the discussion in the house of Agathon that Plato records. Eros is not that which pushes us toward another, but rather it is an attraction. So that eros could embrace such things as love of a friend, a man or a woman, love of art, love of philosophy, love of the good life. Every true and lasting friendship is related to eros. G. K. Chesterton wrote to his future wife, Frances Blogg: "There are four lamps of thanksgiving burning before me. The first that I was born out of the same earth as you. Two, I have tried to love everything in the universe as a remote preparation for loving you. Three, I have never run after strange women. You cannot understand how much this prepares a man for true love. Four, my previous existence ends here. It has led me to you." That is eros. I once asked a man what he would like to be if he could come back to earth two years after he died. He said his wife's second husband. That, too, is eros.

Eros became erotic   *November 21*

After Freud, eros became the erotic, and love became identified with sex. Or rather, we had sex without love. The erotic became merely that which gave pleasure. You drink the water, you forget the glass. There is no communication of person with person. Real love implies the irreplaceability of persons. No one can take the place of a father or a mother, a brother or a sister and so forth. But sex is replaceable. And it has moved in our American life to the mind. It is not just a body phenomenon. That is one of the reasons for the love of pornography. Pornography is a love of the abstract, when the concrete use of the thing has been forgotten. I once met a woman who told me that she paid $250 for a coffee grinder. She paid this sum in order to have this coffee grinder, but she never intended to grind coffee. Well, that is what might be known as coffee pornography. And so when the concrete use of sex is forgotten, and it comes to be used for the purposes of advertising and excitement and so forth, then it becomes pornographic.

The Greeks had a second word for love which was *philia*. This is the love we have for humanity. It was to be irrespective of any class, race, color, or any other distinction. Philia was not just a liking, it was a loving. Now there's a difference between the two. Liking is in the emotions, in the feelings. Loving is in the will. Because liking is in the emotions, the emotions can change, grow dull. But loving is in the will, and is therefore subject to command. Hence our Lord said: "A new commandment I give to you"—a *commandment*— "Love one another as I have loved you." This is the difference between the two.

I can illustrate it by an example. I don't like chicken. Why don't I like chicken? Because when I was a boy, my father used to send us Sheen kids out to one of his farms every weekend and every summer. The tenant farmer, in order to get in good with us, would give us chicken every day except Friday. In the course of my young life, I wrung the necks of 48,632 hens. At night I don't have nightmares, I have night-hens. I have visions of headless chickens squirming in barn-yard dust. So I don't like chicken. But if I go to a retreat and am given chicken, I eat it because I could love it. I don't want to hurt the person in the galley who gave it to me. This is the difference between liking and loving.

Not sensitivity training   *November 23*

Philia is done through the triple communication of love: speech, vision, and touch. That is why to touch someone who is ill or in need is far better, sometimes, than just giving a check. Here I am not speaking of sensitivity training. In a classroom of the University of California, I saw a group of students, boys and girls, sitting around in a circle, in alternate fashion holding hands. They asked: "What do you think of this? See, this is the way we get acquainted with one another. This is what we call sensitivity training."

"Listen," I said, "go out and hold the hand of some wrinkled old man, or some wrinkled old woman. Go out and touch the hand of a leper. Then you'll know whether you love your fellow man."

Christian doctrine or Christian service? *November 24*

The highest degree of *philia* comes through service. When we become exhausted through service, we are always happy and refreshed.

It may very well be that this is where our CCD breaks down. I changed the name to Christian Life, away from Christian Doctrine because I did not like the emphasis on doctrine. Our Blessed Lord said: "If you do my will, you will know my doctrine." He never said, "If you know my doctrine you will do my will." Obedience is the path to knowledge. Obedience prepares for the Spirit: after thirty years of obedience, our Lord received the Spirit. A scientist learns the laws of nature by sitting patiently and obediently before nature to allow it to tell him its secrets. So, if we could introduce not just doctrine, but service, the acting out in the concrete fashion of Christian doctrine, to our children, it would mean much more to them. They would learn the gospels, learn the doctrine of love of neighbor, not just simply from a book, but from self-sacrifice.

The greedy old woman in hell *November 25*

Loving is a very sound evangelical principle as regards humanity. There's a Russian story that says that an angel came once to an old woman in hell and said to her, "If you can think of any one good thing you did during your life, I will let you out of hell." The old lady said, "Well, I once gave a beggar a carrot." "Very well," said the angel, "I will let a carrot down into hell and you get hold of it, and I will pull you out." The old woman was being pulled out, and of course thousands grabbed on to her, and she said, "Get off. This is for me." They all fell back down, including her, because *philia* implies solidarity and community.

The sin of eating alone   *November 26*

I once asked a missionary on a Pacific island what was the greatest virtue of the people. He said, "I can tell you the greatest virtue in terms of the greatest vice. It is the sin of *kaipo*, the sin of eating alone. They would go without food for several days until they could find someone with whom they could share their food."

Strength comes from charity   *November 27*

A Christian mystic from India, Sadhu Sundar Singh, several years ago wanted to go into Tibet to evangelize. He hired a Tibetan guide to take him over the Himalayas. They had gone but a short distance when they became tired and sat on the snow and ice. Then Singh said, "I think I hear someone groaning in the abyss."

The Tibetan said: "Well, what difference does it make? We're almost dead ourselves."

Singh went down, found a man, and dragged him to the base of the Himalayas to a little village. Refreshed by his act of charity, he came back to find the Tibetan guide frozen to death on the ice.

The love called *agape* is sacrificial love. This is the love that we preach and we try to inculcate, not eros or just philia alone, because the philia love will come out of this divine love. Here is an example of how it was practiced. The wife of a friend of mine was one night called downstairs. Her husband was talking to a Nazi. They were Jews who became Christians, Lutherans. And the husband said to the Nazi, "How many Jews have you killed in the last six weeks?"

"About 25,000", he replied.

"In what places?" He mentioned the name of cities. "In this particular village, how many Jews did you kill?"

"I killed all the Jews", he replied.

"Do you feel any remorse?"

"No."

"Do you ever think of asking God for pardon?"

"There isn't any such thing in all the world as forgiveness. There isn't any such thing as God."

My friend said: "Let us see. My wife is asleep upstairs. She has not heard this conversation. I shall call her down." She dressed and came down and he said: "Sabina, this is the man who killed your father and your mother and your three brothers and two sisters."

She looked at him and then threw her arms around his neck and kissed him and said: "God forgives you. I forgive you." And the Nazi threw himself on his knees before the husband and asked him to pray to God for forgiveness. This was the divine forgiving love.

How I failed in love   *November 29*

I will tell you how I failed once. I've failed many times, but this instance was notable. I was visiting lepers in Biluba, Africa.

I had with me 500 silver crucifixes about two inches high. I intended to give each leper a silver crucifix. The first one who came to me had his left arm eaten away by the disease. He held up the stump; there was a rosary around it. He put out his right hand. It was the most foul, fetid, noisome mass of corruption that I ever saw. I held the crucifix above it and dropped it. And it was swallowed up in that volcano of leprosy. And all of a sudden there were 501 lepers in that camp and I was the 501st. For I had taken that symbol of God's identification with man and refused to identify myself with someone who was a thousand times better on the inside than I. Then it came over me the awful thing that I had done. I dug my fingers into his hand and pulled out the crucifix and then pressed it to his hand and so on for all the other 500 lepers. From that time on I learned to love them by touch, by the incarnational principle.

Not to have, but to be had   *November 30*

So the divine love is sacrificial love. Love does not mean to have and to own and to possess. It means to be had and to be owned and to be possessed. It is not a circle circumscribed by self; it is arms outstretched to embrace all humanity within its grasp. No other love is ever going to be a satisfying love. All that we ever get in this world anyway is just a fragment, a fraction of love. We can catch a spark; it is caught up from the great white flame of love which is God. That's all we ever get. And if, to remind us of another love, the spark is so bright, then what must be the flame? It's the cross; it's self-denial, it's victimhood, for this is the gospel of Christ, and we cannot soften him. He is the one who gave his life, and that's the way he measures his love. Greater love than this no man has. When we stay close to that love, day after day, hour after hour, others will begin to feel that love.

December

A missing piece of your heart   *December 1*

This human heart of yours is not perfect in shape as a valentine heart. There's a small piece missing out of the side of your heart and out of every human heart. That is the piece that was torn out of the universal heart of humanity on the cross. When God made your heart and every other heart, he found it so good that he kept a small sample of it in heaven and then sent the rest of it into this world where it would try to fill up all the love it could, but where it would never be really happy, never totally in love, never able to love anyone with a whole heart because it hasn't a whole heart to love with. It will never be happy until it goes back again to God to recover that piece that he has been keeping for it from all eternity.

Marriage is a symbol of the love of God   *December 2*

Every woman promises a man a love that only God can give. And every man promises a woman a love that only God can give. A finite creature cannot bear its yearning of the infinite love any more than a statue of bronze can rest upon the stem of a flower. Men and women are all looking for another kind of love. Today this causes the breakdown of the marriage covenant, which is always the symbol of the divine covenant. When people leave one marriage and seek another, it is like the addition of zeroes, which never, never brings happiness.

The call of Peter*December 3*

When our Lord was driven out of his own home town and came down to the Galilee district, Peter had just come in from fishing all night, and he had caught nothing. When Jesus asked him if he had caught anything, and he said, "Nothing", our Lord said, "Throw your nets into the sea." Now this was a stupid suggestion. It's morning, the sun is up, they're at shore. What does a carpenter know about fishing anyway? According to some texts of the gospel, Simon said, "At your word, master, I will let down a net." He humored the Lord because Jesus knew nothing about fishing. And then came the great catch of fish, and he called Jesus "Lord", no longer master, but Lord. Then he recognized his own sinfulness: "Depart from me, for I am a sinful man."

We are fallen*December 4*

God certainly did not create us this way. We are fallen. All the facts support this view. There is a voice inside our moral conscience that tells us that our immoral and unmoral acts are abnormal. They ought not to be there. There's something wrong in us, something dislocated. God did not make us one way. Or rather, he did make us one way. And we have made ourselves, in virtue of our freedom, in other ways. He wrote the drama; we changed the plot. We are not just animals that failed to evolve into humans. We are humans who have rebelled against the divine. If we are riddles to ourselves, we are not to put the blame on God or on evolution. But we are to put the blame on ourselves. We are not just a mass of corruption, but we bear within ourselves the image of God. We are very much like a man who has fallen into a well. We ought not to be there, and yet we cannot get out. We are sick; we need healing; we need deliverance; we need

liberation, and we know very well that we cannot give this liberation and this freedom to ourselves. We are like a fish on top of the Empire State Building. Somehow or other we are outside of our environment. We cannot swim back into the stream. Someone has to put us back.

Eternity *December 5*

Why must heaven be outside of time? Simply because none of us would want an endless existence on this earth. If it were possible for us to live four hundred years with some kind of vitamin, do you think that we would all swallow them? There would certainly come one moment in our existence when we would want to die. Have you ever been in any one place on this earth that you were absolutely sure would be one in which you would want to spend every day of your life? It is not very likely. The mere extension of time to most of us would probably be a curse instead of a blessing. Then, too, have you ever noticed that your happiest moments have come when eternity almost seems to get inside of your soul? All great inspirations are timeless, and that gives us some suggestion of heaven. Mozart was once asked when he received his inspirations for his great music. He said he saw them all at once in a great heat, a great warmth, a great light. Then there came the succession of notes. So it is in writing a speech. When I prepare a talk, or a telecast, or a book, there comes a moment when the end is seen at the beginning. One cannot write fast enough. There comes to everyone, whether he is good or bad, some dim intimations of immortality such as Wordsworth wrote about. There are, however, men who try to immunize themselves from these thoughts of eternity. They put on a kind of God-proof raincoat, so that the drops of his grace will not get through to them. They shut out eternity.

Too often we think of heaven as being way out there. We draw all kinds of pictures about heaven. Most of them are quite unreal, and because we think of heaven, and even hell, as something that happens to us at the end of time, we keep on postponing it. As a matter of fact, heaven is not way out there; heaven is in here. Hell is not way down there; hell could be inside of a soul. There is no such thing as dying and then going to heaven, or dying and going to hell. You are in heaven already; you are in hell already. I have met people who are in hell. I am sure you have too. I have also seen people with heaven in them. If you ever want to see heaven in a child, look at that child on the day of his first communion. If you want to see how much love is related to heaven, just look at the bride and groom at the altar on the day of the nuptial Mass. Heaven is there; heaven is there because love is there. I have seen heaven in a missionary nun who was spending herself among the lepers. Sometimes you see a virtuous young person and you see heaven there. The beauty of such a person is not put on the outside, it is a kind of imprisoned loveliness that comes from within, as if it were breaking down the bars of flesh in order to find some outward utterance.

A man who wanted to go to hell   *December 7*

I remember once attending a man in a hospital. When I asked him to make his peace with God he said, "I suppose you're going to tell me I'm going to hell."

"No," I said, "I'm not."

"Well," he said, "I want to go to hell."

I replied, "I have never in my life met a man who wanted to go to hell, so I think I will just sit here and watch you go." Of course, I did not intend to let time pass without doing something, but I was absolutely sure that if he had a few minutes to himself, he might change his point of view. So I sat alone with him for twenty minutes. I could see him going through a kind of soul struggle.

Then he said to me, "You really believe there is a hell?"

I asked him, "Do you feel unhappy on the inside? Are you fearful? Is there dread, anxiety? Are all the evil things of your life coming up before you as a specter, a ghost?" Well, it was not long until he made his peace with God.

Why the virgin birth? *December 8*

Our human nature was very much like a polluted stream up until the Incarnation. Imagine a ship, for example, sailing in polluted waters. It wishes to sail in clear waters, but without the pollution coming from one into the other. How could the transfer of the ship be made except by a lock? So the ship in the foul waters would be put into a lock where there would be a separation of waters, then the ship would be raised to the level of the unpolluted waters. Now the Immaculate Conception and the virgin birth were that lock. The pollution stopped because there was no union of man and woman. It was simply woman alone who gave a human nature to Christ and began the new humanity.

Heaven grows in us *December 9*

Heaven is very close to us because heaven is related to a good life in much the same way that an acorn is related to an oak. An acorn is bound to become an oak. He who does not have heaven in his heart now will never go to heaven, and he who has hell in his heart when he dies will go to hell. We must not think that heaven is related to a good life in the same way a gold medal is related to study. Because a gold medal need not follow study. It is purely extrinsic to study. Rather, heaven is related to a good and virtuous life in just the same way that knowledge is related to study. One necessarily follows the other. Hell is not related to an evil life in the same way that spanking is related to an act of disobedience. Spanking need not follow an act of disobedience. As a matter of fact, it rarely follows disobedience today. Rather, it is related in the same way that corruption is related to death. One necessarily follows the other. Therefore, heaven is not just a long way off; we are not to postpone it. It is here. That is to say, it begins here.

Like the Israelites in the desert   *December 10*

Heaven starts here, but it doesn't end here. We just get faint glimpses of it now and then. If we postpone the thought of heaven until the moment we die, we will be very much like the Israelites during their wanderings in the desert. They were at one time within about eleven days of the promised land. It took only three weeks for them to make the journey from Egypt to the promised land, but because of their disobedience, their failures, their backsliding, and their rebellion against Moses, it took them forty years to get into the promised land. That forty years represents a pilgrimage in the lives of most of us. We make progress, and then we slip back. Thank heavens we have a merciful Lord who puts up with us and forgives us seventy times seven. Therefore, time is necessary in order to gain heaven, but the lapse of time itself does not bring me to heaven. What brings me to heaven is how I live, how I die.

Now we come to what our Lord said about heaven. It was the night of the Last Supper. Jesus gathered about him all his apostles—poor, weak, frail men. He washed their feet. He was facing the agony in the garden, and that terrible betraying kiss of Judas, and even the denial of Peter himself. One would think that all the talk would be about himself. Certainly, when we have trials, that is what we think about. But our Lord thought about the apostles. He saw the sadness in their faces, and he said, "Be not troubled, do not be sad, I go to prepare a place for you. In my father's house there are many mansions." How did he know about the Father's house? He came from there. That was his home. Now preparing to go back home, he tells them about the Father's house and he says, "I go to prepare a place for you." God never does anything for us without great preparation. He made a garden for Adam, as only God knows how to make a garden beautiful. Then, when the Jews came into the promised land, he prepared the land for them. He said he would give them houses full of good things, houses which they never built. He said that he would give them vineyards and olive trees which they never planted. Just so, he goes to prepare a place for us. Why? Simply because we were not made for heaven; we were made for earth. Man, by sin, spoiled the earth, and God came down from heaven in order to help us remake it. After having redeemed us, he said that he would now give us heaven, so we got all this: the earth, and heaven too.

What heaven is like   *December 12*

Heaven is social; it is a fellowship. In some places, heaven is called a country, to indicate its vastness. It is called a city, to suggest the number of its inhabitants. It is called a kingdom, to suggest order and harmony. It is called a paradise in order to tell of its delights. And it is called the Father's house in order to indicate its eternity and its permanence of love and peace. In order to be perfectly happy after the end of the world, we will have to have our bodies with us because our bodies have done a great deal for the salvation of our souls. There we will meet, in the fullness of the communion of saints, all those who were our friends on earth.

I'll see you in heaven   *December 13*

Just think of some great moment in life when you really enjoyed the thrill of living. Then go back and think of some great moment when somebody told you a truth or you made a study of a great mystery and finally understood it. Then go to another moment of your life when you had a great ecstasy of love and you wanted it to go on and on and on. Now suppose you could take this moment of life, raise it up to a focal point where it became the far deepest truth, lift it to infinity until it became the moment of the ecstasy of truth, and take that moment of love and eternalize it so that it became the Holy Spirit. Well, that gives some dim suggestion of what heaven is. It is perfect life. It is perfect truth. It is perfect love. I am not afraid of going to hell, I am only afraid of losing love, that's all. That's divine love; that's Christ. The reason I want to go to heaven is because I want to be with love. Oh, there will be surprises there, many of them. First of all, there will be many people there whom we never expected to see there. There will also be a number of people absent who we thought would be there. Finally, there will be one great surprise, the greatest of all, that you and I are there. I'll see you in heaven.

Hell is close to heaven *December 14*

Just imagine a perfect day in springtime: birds are singing, the rushing river sparkles nearby, mountains are seen in the distance. All nature seems to be reflecting the divine power of the Creator. In all of this peace one man goes to a river where fish live in contentment because they are wet. He takes one fish out of that water and holds it up. Where is that fish at that moment? That fish is in hell. See how close he is to heaven. Everything else is heavenly, but he is in hell because he was made to be wet. As that fish was made to be wet, we were meant to be with God. Then we will be in heaven.

As sin abounded, grace abounded more *December 15*

Let's go back and think of all the repercussions of the sin of Adam. There isn't an Arab; there isn't an American; there isn't a European; there isn't an Asiatic in the world who does not feel within himself something of the complexes, the contradictions, the contrarieties, the civil wars, the rebellions inside of his human nature which he has inherited from Adam. We all struggle against temptation. Why? Simply because our human nature was disordered in the beginning. There is a terrific monotony about human nature. You must not think that you are the only one in the world who has a tortured soul. Now if the sin of Adam had so many repercussions in every human being that has ever lived, shall we deny that the Incarnation of our Blessed Lord has had a greater repercussion? Can it be that the sin of one man can have greater effects and disorder in human nature than the Incarnation of the Son of God has in ordering all humanity? That is why I say that everybody in the world is implicitly Christian. Some may not become Christians, but that is not the fault of Christ. He took their humanity upon himself.

In a certain sense the human nature of our Blessed Lord was unlimited. It could embrace within itself all the human natures of the world. In other words, that human nature of Christ represented to a great extent the human nature of every single person who has ever lived. You read his genealogy in Matthew and in Luke, and you will find saints, but you will also find sinners. There was a bend sinister in his pedigree. We find Gentile women like Ruth; we find a public sinner like Rahab. These were typical of the humanity that Christ assumed into himself when he became incarnate. Every human being that would ever be born until the end of time was incorporated into this humanity. Hence there's not a Buddhist, not a Confucianist, not a communist, not a sinner, not a saint who is not in some way part of this human nature of Christ. You are in it. Your next-door neighbor is in it. Every persecutor of the Church is in it. When, therefore, we are puzzled about how other people are saved, we need only realize that here is implicitly all salvation, all men in Christ.

United and separated   *December 17*

There are two verses in scripture, one from Isaiah and the other from the epistle to the Hebrews, which seem to be contradictory. Isaiah says that our Lord was reckoned with the transgressors, or sinners. The epistle to the Hebrews says that he was separated from sinners. He was one with them and at the same time not with them. He was reckoned with sinners, inasmuch as in his human nature he took upon himself all the penalties of sin. He was separated simply because he was God and also because, even in his human nature, he was like us in all things, save sin.

Our Savior is our judge

When our Lord comes, it will not be just to judge the one circumscribed area of the earth in which he labored and revealed himself. It will be to reveal himself and to judge all nations and all empires. When that time is, nobody knows. He refuses to tell us. He only says that it will be sudden, like a flash of lightning. He, the Savior, is the judge. What a beautiful way to have a judgment. Can you imagine any earthly judge saying to a criminal before him: you were guilty, I am going to take all of your sins and crimes upon myself. I will suffer for you. What a judge he would be! But our Blessed Lord took upon himself all of our sins as we stood before the bar of divine justice, and he who suffered for us will come to judge us. What a judgment it will be when we will see one who loved us so much.

Nuptials

December 19

What is the idea that runs all through scripture? It is nuptials. The covenant is based on nuptials. As we used to say in the old marriage ceremony, "Not even the flood took it away, not even sin." There was the nuptials of man and woman in the garden of Eden, the nuptials of Israel and God in the Old Testament. In the prophet Hosea: "I your Creator am your husband." God is the husband of Israel. In that beautiful passage of the book of Hosea, God tells Hosea to marry a prostitute, a worthless woman. She leaves him, betrays him, commits adultery, has children by other men, and when the heart of Hosea is broken, God says, "Hosea, take her back, take her back. She's the symbol of Israel. Israel has been my unworthy spouse, but I love Israel, and I will never let her go." Hosea taking back the prostitute is the symbol of God's love for his *qahal*, his church of the Old Testament. Now we come to new nuptials, the nuptials of divinity and humanity in our Blessed Mother.

Why Christ came to earth   *December 20*

You may remember from Shakespeare the famous speech of Mark Anthony over Caesar. He said, "I will show you sweet Caesar's wounds, poor, poor dumb mouths and bid them speak for me." Instead of showing you Caesar's wounds, I shall show you the wounds of Christ, who is both God and man, the only one who ever came to this earth to die and to conquer it. You and I came into the world to live; he came into the world to offer his life for us. And so he founded a new type of religion. All other religions, without exception, go from man to God, either by contemplation or by a kind of mortification and self-denial. One, for example, is the eight-fold path of Buddha. But with our Blessed Lord, religion comes from God to man. We need help and, particularly, redemption from sin.

Nature is in childbirth   *December 21*

In this late day of creation we are troubled by pollution, and nature seems to turn against us. Will nature ever be completely liberated? Yes. Scripture tells us it is waiting for the liberation of the sons of God. When the number of the elect is completed, then there will be a new heaven and a new earth. St. Paul has a beautiful description of that in the eighth chapter of Romans. "For the created universe waits with eager expectation for God's Son to be revealed. It was made the victim of frustration, not by its own choice." Nature did not become rebellious because it willed it, but because of him who made it so—because of us. And always there was hope, because the universe itself is to be freed from the shackles of mortality and enter upon the liberty and splendor of the children of God. "Up to the present, we know, the whole created universe groans in all of its parts, as if in the pangs of childbirth." Just think of it. We hardly think of nature that way. No poet has ever sung about nature being like a woman in childbirth. And yet here it is. We can hardly wait. Each sunrise, each sunset: nature is expectant. When will men serve God and the number of the elect be complete?

Heaven was not empty   *December 22*

When we say that God became man, we do not mean to say that heaven was empty. That would be to think of heaven as a kind of a space, like a room that was twenty by thirty feet. When God came to this world, he did not leave heaven empty. When he came to this world, he was not shaved down, whittled down to human proportions. Rather, Christ was the life of God dwelling in human flesh. St. Thomas Aquinas includes a very beautiful description of this in one of his hymns. He said, "The heavenly Word proceeding forth, yet leaving not the Father's side."

One chance in millions   *December 23*

A Jewish scholar who became a Christian and who knew the Old Testament very well and all of the traditions of the Jews, said that at the time of Christ the rabbis had gathered together 456 prophecies concerning the Messiah, the Christ, the conqueror of evil who was to be born and to enter into a new covenant with mankind. Suppose the chances of any one prophecy being fulfilled by accident, say the place where he would be born, was one in a hundred. Then, if two prophecies were fulfilled, the chances would be one in a thousand. If three prophecies were to coincide in Christ, that would be one in ten thousand. If four, one in a hundred thousand. If five, one in a million. Now if all of these prophecies were fulfilled in Christ, what would be the chance of them all concurring at the appointed moment, not only in place but also in time, as was foretold by the prophet Daniel? Take a pencil and write on a sheet of paper the numeral 1, and draw a line beneath it. Under the line write 84, and after 84, if you have time, write 126 zeros. That is the chance of all of the prophecies of Christ being fulfilled. It runs into millions and millions, trillions and trillions.

No room in the inn   *December 24*

Mary is now with child, awaiting birth, and Joseph is full of expectancy as he enters the city of his own family. He searched for a place for the birth of him to whom heaven and earth belonged. Could it be that the Creator would not find room in his own creation? Certainly, thought Joseph, there would be room in the village inn. There was room for the rich; there was room for those who were clothed in soft garments; there was room for everyone who had a tip to give to the innkeeper. But when finally the scrolls of history are completed down to the last word of time, the saddest line of all will be: "There was no room in the inn." No room in the inn, but there was room in the stable. The inn was the gathering place of public opinion, the focal point of the world's moods, the rendezvous of the worldly, the rallying place of the popular and the successful. But there's no room in the place where the world gathers. The stable is a place for outcasts, the ignored and the forgotten. The world might have expected the Son of God to be born in an inn; a stable would certainly be the last place in the world where one would look for him. The lesson is: divinity is always where you least expect to find it. So the Son of God made man is invited to enter into his own world through a back door.

What Jesus did on Christmas

In the epistle to the Philippians we read: "For the divine nature was his from the first"—Christ was always God—"Yet he did not think to snatch at equality with God." Who snatched at equality with God? Satan did. And Adam did when Satan told him he would be like God. But he who is God by nature did not snatch at equality with God, but "made himself nothing." *Nothing.* The old translation was "He emptied himself." In theology this is called *kenosis.* God emptied himself; he made himself a nothing, "assuming the nature of a slave"—not merely of a servant. The Greek word is *doulos.* The word *doulos* is used about forty-seven times by our Lord in the New Testament. A slave does hard work; a slave does dirty work. Assuming the nature of a slave, "bearing human likeness, revealed in human shape, he humbled himself and in obedience accepted even death—death on the cross." So he emptied himself. This verse is Christmas, "He emptied himself."

What was it like for God to be a man?

What did it mean for God to become man? Suppose you were very much concerned about the way dogs acted in the city of Washington. They barked at postmen; they snapped at mailmen; they refused to be housebroken. And you loved dogs. So you emptied yourself of your body, and you took your mind and put it into the body of a dog. This would involve, first of all, the humiliation of having a mind which far transcended your organism. You would have a mind which could scan the stars, but you would follow instinct. You could speak, but you would only bark. The other humiliation would be to spend the rest of your life with dogs—sick-and-tired of hydrants. And then in the end, they turn on you and tear you to pieces. If it would be hard for us to become a dog, to teach dogs to be good, what was it for God to become a man, humbling himself, making himself a zero and then taking upon himself all of our sins?

The cave of humility   *December 27*

Exiled from the earth, our Lord is born under the earth, for the stable was in a cave. He was the first caveman of recorded history, and there he shook the earth to its very foundations. Because he's born in a cave, all who wish to see him must bend, must stoop, and the stoop is the mark of humility. The proud refuse to stoop. Therefore they miss divinity. Those, however, who are willing to risk bending their egos to go into that cave, find that they are not in a cave at all; but they are in a universe where sits a babe on his mother's lap, the babe who made the world.

The gifts of the Magi   *December 28*

The Magi came from the East. How did they know about Christ? Probably from the prophecy of Daniel concerning the seventy weeks of years; they counted the revolution of the stars. In any case, they knew, and they brought gold because he was king, incense because he was a priest, but also myrrh. That's the way he was buried, with a hundred pounds of spices and myrrh. What would our mothers have thought if the neighbors brought in embalming fluid when we were born? Everywhere there was the shadow of suffering.

Obedience gives us faith

What does obedience do for us? Obedience gives us faith. How does the scientist learn the laws of nature? Does he command nature, or does the scientist sit passively and read the book of nature? Are we reacting against Christ and his Church, or are we accepting its authority? Faith comes from that kind of submission. Remember that when our Blessed Lord was born, Herod consulted the scribes, the theologians. He said to the scribes, "Where is Christ to be born?" The theologians knew their scripture. They said, "He is to be born in Bethlehem." Did they go? There was not a single scribe at the crib—not one. But they knew. Our faith today can be a kind of a credal assent, instead of a living act of the will, conscious of the fact that we are submitting to Christ, as Christ submitted to the heavenly Father. Scripture tells us how closely faith is related to obedience. Notice, too, that at the crib, only two classes of people found their way to Christ when he came to this earth: the very simple, and the very learned—the shepherds who knew that they knew nothing, and the wise men who knew that they did not know everything; never the man who thought that he knew.

Our virgin birth

I cannot see why a Christian should be in the least bit troubled about the virgin birth, because there's a virgin birth in us all. Everyone who becomes a Christian has Christ in him. Christ is born and conceived in everyone by baptism. There is first of all the renewal crisis in the intellect so that, as Paul says, we "put on the mind of Christ". He is in the will, as grace and power. And he is in our body, because our body becomes the temple of God. The convert (it's easy to understand in a convert because one can always distinguish the before and after state) can often say: "Oh, yes, at this precise date I heard the word of God. And the Word was born in me so that I have his truth and his grace, and he's living inside of my body." There is conception by perception, conception by the hearing of the word of God.

Dr. Updike, upstairs   *December 31*

There was a young doctor in the southern part of the United States who took care of poor Mexican mothers and children. One day he became engaged. The young woman prepared a pre-engagement party, but the night of the party the doctor was called to care for a Mexican woman who was dying in childbirth. He did not go to the party; he saved the mother, and he also saved the child. The girl broke off the engagement. The doctor had his office above a grocery store, with a sign down below telling that his office was on the second floor. When he died after living in poverty, people wondered how he could ever be repaid for what he had done. Finally, they took the sign from the grocery store at the foot of the stairs, and they put it on his coffin. Everyone who saw his nameplate understood what his life of pain had brought him to: "Doctor Updike, upstairs."

ACKNOWLEDGMENTS

Grateful acknowledgment is made to Ministr-O-Media, Inc. for permission to make selections from the following tapes to which they own the copyright: "The Church Today", "The Nemesis of Mediocrity", "What God Has Done for Us", "My Role in Reconciliation", "The Holy Sacrifice of the Mass", "The Holy Eucharist and the Gospels", The Lord Asks for an Hour", "Treasures and Pots", "Sin Is in the Blood", "Judas", "Demonic", "Our Skolops", "Fools for Christ's Sake", "The Holy Spirit", "The Eternal Freshness of the Wounds of Christ", "Three Words for Love", "The Fall and Resurrection of Peter", "Christ: His Passion and Death— Desecration of the Temple, Last Supper and the Agony, Death March to Jerusalem, Mary Magdalene and Judas, The Crucifixion, and The Meaning of the Resurrection", "The Answers to the Seven Burdens of Life (First Word: 'Am I Sick or a Sinner?'; Second Word: 'How do I take Pain?'; Third Word: 'Do I Need the Feminine in Religion?'; Fourth Word: 'Did Christ Think of the Atheists?'; Fifth Word: 'Do I Need a Love Beyond Love?'; Sixth Word: 'Should I Come Down from the Cross?'; Seventh Word: 'Do I Have Any Scars?')", "Cor ad Cor Loquitur", "Good Friday 1979: 'Spectators'". Copyright to this material remains the property of Ministr-O-Media. All rights reserved. Reprinted by permission.

Grateful acknowledgment is also made to The Society for the Propagation of the Faith and to Keep the Faith, Inc., for selections from the "Ye Shall Know the Truth" series, originally published on records entitled "Life Is Worth Living".